THE 5–10-YEAR-OLD CHILD

THE 5–10-YEAR-OLD CHILD

Abrahão H. Brafman

LONDON AND NEW YORK

First published 2010 by Karnac Books Ltd.

Published 2018 by Routledge
2 Park Square, Milton Park, Abingdon, Oxon OX14 4RN
711 Third Avenue, New York, NY 10017, USA

Routledge is an imprint of the Taylor & Francis Group, an informa business

British Library Cataloguing in Publication Data

A C.I.P. for this book is available from the British Library

ISBN: 9781855757035 (pbk)

Edited, designed and produced by The Studio Publishing Services Ltd
www.publishingservicesuk.co.uk
e-mail: studio@publishingservicesuk.co.uk

CONTENTS

ABOUT THE AUTHOR

Dr Abrahão H. Brafman worked as a Consultant Child and Adolescent Psychiatrist in the NHS until his retirement. He is a qualified psychoanalyst of adults and children, and gave seminars on infant observation for trainees of the British Psychoanalytic Society and other training institutions. For many years he ran a weekly meeting for under-fives and their parents at Queen Mary's Hospital, Roehampton, London. He has published two books based on his work with children and parents: *Untying the Knot* (Karnac, 2001) and *Can You Help Me?* (Karnac, 2004), as well as a series of papers on various clinical topics. For several years, under the sponsorship of the Winnicott Trust, he ran weekly clinical seminars for medical students at the University Hospital Medical School, Department of Psychotherapy.

Full-time schooling in Britain starts after the child is five years old. This is the point where parents have to accept that their child is out of their sight for most of the day. Some parents will feel free to devote their time to work or other favoured pursuits, but others may feel quite lost, as if deprived of a valued *raison d'être*. The period from five up to ten years of age also represents a time when most children are more difficult to reach. Some children find difficulty in adjusting to the ethos of a primary school, but at the same time they appear to lose their ability to confide in the parents. The "open", spontaneous under-five becomes a reserved, elusive child and, even if they know that this is not a sign of pathology, some parents do struggle to rediscover their younger child.

Puberty signals further changes, both physical and emotional, but this book focuses on that period that psychoanalysts call "latency years", a colourful description of years when the child's impulses and feelings appear to become dormant, as if he wanted to isolate himself from the world.

The literature describing the developmental stages that lead the infant to adulthood contains two aspects that deserve to be made explicit and discussed. One is the difference between references to the *actual* infant, as distinct from those focusing on the *reconstructed* infant (Stern, 1995); the other follows from this one and involves the degree of experience that the authors have of direct, close involvement with infants and children. It is very easy to ignore these features, but, once aware of them, one realizes how important they are and the degree to which they affect the views put forward by the authors.

Over the years, I have met many analysts and psychotherapists to discuss the observation of infants or actual clinical work with children. I came to recognize that some of these students or qualified professionals spoke about the infant or child they were involved with in a manner that suggested a sense of distance and coldness; they seemed to be reporting the finding of something they had read or heard about. I could not pick up the tone of delight and warmth that one experiences when discovering something new in an object that one feels close to, the sense of excitement and discovery that an individual object engenders when approached with a background of recognition and familiarity. In other words, having been close to other infants or children, the gratifying discovery that this is not "just another infant", but a new, different, special infant, with his own unique characteristics.

Eventually, it occurred to me to ask these students what previous experience they had had with young children and I was surprised to find that the infant they observed or the child they were treating was the first child they had ever come so close to. These were professionals who had trained to work with adults, and it became clear that the images they had of "an infant" or "a child" had been gained from their studies. I later found that most people who decided to train in the analytic approach to children opted for the child psychotherapy training, while those who chose the psychoanalytic training were aiming to work with adults. This may well be the explanation for the failure of all the efforts made by so many analysts to persuade their trainees to get involved with children or, at least, with the study of children.

Anna Freud (1972) saw the child as a live field of research and she believed that "child analysis . . . opened up the possibility to check up on the correctness of reconstructions in adult analysis" (p. 153). And yet, analysts of adults remained more or less aloof from child analysis, almost as if it were an inferior type of professional occupation . . . It was difficult not to suspect that most analysts vastly preferred the childhood images which emerged from their interpretations to the real children in whom they remained uninterested. [*ibid.*]

Hannah Segal (1972) shared Anna Freud's views:

In our institute in Great Britain we had for years lectures on child analysis and clinical seminars, which were compulsory for all students. Unfortunately, we are going through one of our periodic great upheavals and reorganization, and I find to my horror that the child has been thrown out with the bath water: the course of child analysis for the ordinary candidate has disappeared, I hope only very temporarily. [p. 160]

To help a professional to obtain true, thorough familiarity with the growing child, she listed what she saw as her

minimal requirements: first, full integration of theory of psycho-analytic knowledge derived from the analysis of children in teach-ing; secondly, baby and child observation; and thirdly, attendances at lectures and clinical seminars on child analysis irrespective of whether the candidate is treating children himself. [*ibid.*]

In fact, infant observation has been the only one of these disci-plines that has been (virtually) universally adopted as part of the training in adult analysis and psychotherapy. However, analysing the reports of students and reading the available literature, we can recognize the effect of the preconceptions with which the observers approach infant and parent(s). We can only *see* what *we make* of that which our eyes show us. This is not pathological; it is an inevitable fact. Whichever one of our senses is stimulated, some perception is formed and immediately interpreted in line with previous experi-ences. Presumably, each and every one of us is able to spot a sen-sorial stimulus not previously met, but if some stop and try to make sense of it, others quickly ignore it, choosing to concentrate on more familiar perceptions and interpretations. Of course, nobody reaches adulthood without having been involved with children of all ages, but there is a major difference between taking an interest, dev-eloping a relationship, and warming up to children and, instead, approaching children as no more than an object of study.

Friends, colleagues, acquaintances, relatives of all ages arouse feelings and images of various degrees of clarity in our minds and we are usually able to describe their qualities and attributes as individuals. But, on becoming a student, there is a powerful qualitative change in our frame of mind and we move on to learn about and search for group characteristics; indeed, this is a response to what most teachers expect from their trainees. In zoology, we learn of species, races, genders, etc., much as in psychology we discover all kinds of classifications of appearance, behaviours, etc. Since medicine has "diagnosis" as the primary goal in the process of investigation of the individual patient, the student has to work hard to learn the relevant data to consider when making his "differential diagnosis", i.e., having considered all *possible* illnesses that *might* be affecting that particular individual, deciding which one is, in fact, producing the clinical phenomena found in that particular patient.

And here lies the problem I wanted to define and focus on. Meeting an infant or a child, we are flooded with images and possible interpretations of what *that child*'s appearance, behaviour, utterances, etc., are supposed to indicate. But, having examined each and every one of these *impressions*, we still have to admit that these are no more than interpretations based on our previous life experiences. Only a closer interaction with the particular child will help us to clarify which of our hypotheses are in fact correct, and, at last, recognize and define the specific cluster of conscious and unconscious thoughts and emotions experienced by the child that lead to its expressed, manifest behaviour and utterances.

The reports of students on their observations of infants demonstrate very clearly the degree to which their descriptions reflect the theoretical framework they are being trained in. Indeed, their personal opinions also influence what they perceive, and only when they give a detailed enough description of their observations will other students be able to recognize other possible ways of interpreting what has been observed. Two examples may illustrate this point:

A seven-month-old baby was described as particularly unresponsive to the mother's ministrations. The student, in fact, at times considered the mother's behaviour as a possible cause of the baby's responses. Taking a broader view of the three visits under discussion, the other students in the group questioned the assessment of their colleague. After some discussion, it occurred to me to ask whether he might be considering the baby's behaviour as an early sign of autism; rather hesitantly, he admitted this was the case. This led to a major change in the focus of the discussion. Subsequent visits led to reports of a normally developing baby, with a mother who seemed to treat him in a very normal manner.

A ten-week-old baby was described as "attacking the mother's nipple in an oral sadistic" manner and, accordingly, producing pain and a withdrawal reaction in the mother. When the student visited the family the following week, the baby was reported as sucking quite normally the mother's breast. The students in the group were, obviously, puzzled, and asked about the destructive oral instincts of the baby. The reporting student, rather timidly, answered that the mother had been visited a few days earlier by a breastfeeding counsellor.

As infants learn to speak and to convey their feelings in a more understandable manner, it becomes easier to make contact with them and gradually learn to understand how they are experiencing life in the world around them. But, predictably, this is easier said than done! Parents, teachers, and doctors find it much easier to TELL the child what they think than to find a way of enabling the child to express what, in fact, are his experiences. Teaching, reassuring, ignoring, comforting, pacifying—or punishing—a child is infinitely easier than conveying to that child that one is interested in discovering what is exciting, worrying, bothering, or frightening him/her.

The parents of a twelve-year-old boy were worried by his behaviour, his refusal to discuss anything with them. School reports were satisfactory, but the parents worried that the boy might be developing some kind of pathological aloofness. I saw the boy on his own and found no sign of the behaviour reported by the parents. I suggested to the parents that I should meet the boy a few more times, but I reassured them that I had not detected any indication of incipient pathology in their son. I wondered whether the behaviour at home might be a pattern developed within the child–parents relationship and inquired what image they had of their interactions with the boy in his earlier years. After some thought, the father recounted that when the boy was four years old he told him one day that he "knew that God created the earth". Father said this was good and continued doing what he was involved with. But, after a few minutes, the boy asked him, "Do you want me to tell you how it is that I know?" The father felt embarrassed, and asked the boy to tell him. "Because there was no ground for anyone to stand on, so only a God could have done it". I suggested that that episode might have remained in the boy's mind as a warning that, in principle, his father was not interested to learn of his thoughts.

If I had only seen the boy by himself, I would not have heard of this episode. Individual sessions would probably reveal his inability to feel free and spontaneous when addressing his father and perhaps he might be helped not to extend this sense of intimidation to his relationship with other men. But if the father can realize the impact his responses have on his son, this may lead him to develop a different pattern of responses to the son. Broadening our picture, we have here examples of keeping an open mind when approaching a child and his parents. The student who thought he was observing an autistic child could recognize the extent to which his initial impressions were influencing his subsequent analysis of his data; the student who thought she had found evidence of Klein's theories regarding the destructive aspects of the oral instincts could take into account the subsequent piece of evidence that strongly argued against her interpretation of the baby's behaviour. The memory put forward by the father of the twelve-year-old boy is a powerful piece of evidence of the importance at all ages of environmental factors shaping a child's mode of relating to his environment.

These arguments and examples aim to depict an approach to child development where the emphasis is on the actual personal experience of each child and his parents, rather than on a particular body of theories built to explain human development. The emphasis is on the richness and freedom that a sense of doubt can create, rather than on the advocacy of dogmatic certainty. Instead of starting from the theoretical and searching for the evidence that will substantiate it, we are choosing an approach where we aim to understand the personal experience of the child and of his parents, and gradually build a picture of the development of their interactions.

The concept of instinctual impulses is well accepted in all areas of biology, but in the analytic world it has become attached to other psychoanalytic concepts to an extent that, to my mind, is difficult to justify. For example, the concepts of self and object images are most useful to evaluate the level of development of an infant's ego, but when it is postulated that instincts can influence the formation of object images *in utero*, I consider this the type of hypothesis that demands faith for its acceptance, since we do not have the equipment to evaluate its validity. The episode quoted above of the observer who claimed to have found evidence of how hostile impulses had led an infant to attack its bad maternal object is an example of this particular application of the concept of inborn instincts.

The opposite extreme is represented by the theories that claim that the infant's personality is the result of the environment in which he grows up. Needless to say, all of these theories will always include comments on the importance of other factors in shaping the infant's development, but not much notice is given to these "other" factors in the description of the developing infant and child. Predictably, analysts will develop their clinical approach in line with the theoretical framework they favour. For example, analysts who maintain that psychopathology originates from early infancy mothering will see early developmental pathology in the patient's material and, correspondingly, attempt to offer a more effective mothering experience.

The authors of the books in this series follow a balanced view of these various theories. There is a refreshing lack of dogmatic views and a high dose of good sense, where theories are respected and quoted, always making sure that a reader can find enough material to form his own view on the validity of the interpretations put forward.

Each book in this series focuses on a particular age range of a child's development. The emphasis is on the description of the typical ways in which the child, at each of these stages, experiences himself in his world. As he develops, the child has different needs, abilities, and resources that underlie his interaction with parents, relatives, and the world at large. Our objective is to illustrate how these unfolding characteristics of the child influence and are influenced by the people in his world. It is only careful and (usually) long-term observation that will allow us to identify elements in the infant's or child's behaviour that are likely to be part of his inborn personality.

Whenever considering a particular individual, it is not difficult to put forward hypotheses about the origins of his various characteristic features, but the converse is virtually impossible. However refined our powers of observation, we are quite incapable of predicting what effects the course of time will produce on an individual. Here lies the special fascination of studying infants and children, where all the time we are surprised by some piece of behaviour we would not have managed to predict.

Meeting the child and his parents, we have to explore the patterns of the relationship they have with each other, and it is virtually impossible to establish what is cause and what is effect in the way they treat each other. Through their words and behaviour, child and parents continuously confirm each other's expectations and keep a self-perpetuating vicious circle going, where each of them feels totally justified in his/her views of him/herself and each other. However, if we find a way of enabling a child to reveal his private thoughts and feelings, we can sometimes discover that these do not quite match his usual statements: most children learn to sense and respect how each parent expects them to behave and what to say, when and where.

All the authors in this series follow a theoretical framework that maintains the importance of emotional and intellectual factors of which we may be unconscious at a particular time. They also follow the theory that individuals are continuously influenced by their experiences—past and present—both those originating in the person's mind and those resulting from interactions with other people. This approach is referred to as a "dynamic" view of the human personality. However, all our authors are aware of the existence of factors in our make-up that appear not to be amenable to change. In fact, we are privileged in having a specific volume in the series that addresses the issue of disadvantage. Given appropriate professional help, such children can improve their capacity to deal with life, but in many cases it will be difficult to predict the extent of this change and, equally important, to determine whether the child acquires new coping mechanisms or, instead, structural changes are achieved.

These differences are significant, not just from a scientific point of view, but also in terms of what we, the professionals, convey to the parents about our assessment of each child. When a child has a structural, inborn or acquired problem, we owe it to the parents to make very clear that, in the course of time, they have learnt of the child's abilities and limitations and found ways of taking these into account when looking after the child. In other words, that some of the child's problems are not the result of their upbringing, but of some factor that is not always easy to pinpoint. When there is no such physical, organic, non-dynamic factor, we can indeed assume we are facing a dynamic problem, but even then it can be difficult to predict the extent to which our therapeutic efforts will achieve change in the presenting problems. This is, in fact, the most difficult challenge that a consultant faces each time he assesses a new child.

It is not rare that each parent will present a quite different reading of what he considers the child's problems to be. Needless to say, the same can be found when considering any issue in the life of an ordinary family. The baby cries and the mother thinks he is hungry, while the father may feel that here is an early warning of a child who will wish to control his parents' lives. The toddler refuses some particular food and the mother resents this early sign of rebellion, while the father will claim that the child is actually showing he can discriminate between pleasant and undesirable flavours. The five-year-old demands a further hour of TV watching and the mother agrees he should share a programme she happens to enjoy, while the father explodes at the pointlessness of trying to instil a sense of discipline in the house. By the time the child reaches puberty or adolescence, these clashes are a matter of daily routine . . . From a practical point of view, it is important to recognize that there is no question of ascertaining which parent is right or which one is wrong: within their personal frame of reference, they are both right. The problem with such disagreements is that, whatever happens, the child will always be agreeing with one of them and opposing the other. But, at this point, I wish to emphasize the obvious fact that each parent reaches his interpretation of the child's behaviour in line with his upbringing and his personality, his view of himself in the world, his past and present experiences, some of which are conscious and most of them unconscious. But—what about the child in question?

It is not part of ordinary family life that a child should be asked what *his* explanation is for the piece of behaviour that led to the situation where the parents disagreed on its interpretation. And, anyway, when he is asked about this, there is a fair chance that, very quickly, one or both parents will challenge him and utter the famous line, "Really? I know your antics! Pull the other one! What you really wanted is . . .". It is just not common to find parents (adults in general, perhaps?) interested and able to discover a child's private justification for his behaviour. Sometimes, the child fails to find the words to explain himself, occasionally he is driven to say what he believes the parent wants to hear, at other times his words sound too illogical to be believed; somehow, the myth has grown that only a professional will have the capacity to fathom out the child's motives and intentions.

Each family will have its own style of approaching their child. It is simply unavoidable that each individual child will have his development influenced (note: not determined, but affected) by the responses his behaviour brings out in his parents. It is, however, quite difficult for parents to appreciate the precise developmental abilities achieved by their child. No child can operate, cope with life, respond to stimuli beyond his particular abilities at any particular point in time. And this is THE point addressed in the present series of books. We try to portray the various stages in the child's cognitive, intellectual, emotional development and how these unfolding stages affect not only his experience of himself, but also how he perceives and responds to the world in which he lives. We hope that this approach will help parents and professionals to gauge how best to make contact with the child and reach an understanding of his feelings and behaviour.

References

Freud, A. (1972). Child analysis as a sub-speciality of psychoanalysis. *International Journal of Psychoanalysis*, 53: 151–156.
Segal, H. (1972). The role of child analysis in the general psychoanalytical training. *International Journal of Psychoanalysis*, 53: 157–161.
Stern, D. (1995). *The Motherhood Constellation*. New York: Basic Books.

Introduction

The fifth birthday represents an important landmark in a child's development. He is now ready to start full-time primary school, and we no longer speak of a baby or a little child; instead, we refer to the boy or the girl. The charm and innocence, or the stubbornness and belligerence, that characterized the under-five and led us to endless tests of our self-control now gives place to someone who seems much more self-contained. His personality characteristics remain the same, but, as his horizons become wider and his experiences outside the home increase exponentially, he seems to become more reserved, more difficult to approach and share things with. Sometimes, ordinary questions are ignored or responded to with some apparently unrelated answer. Occasionally, the child will move away even while someone is speaking to him. At times, being told not to do something, the child will move on to do precisely what he had set out to do. But, as a rule, none of these attitudes carry the appearance of hostility or of a deliberate wish to antagonize the adult involved. This is a child trying to make sense of his new experiences, adapting to new people and places, while preserving his link to his earlier environment. The adult can feel frustrated and impatient, but, when moved to protest, we tend to use words of exasperation rather than plain anger. There exists an unspoken understanding that the child needs time to adjust to his new pattern of life. However, not all over-fives are like this and we do find some who seem to blend into the new pattern of life and carry on with their home life as if no major change had taken place. They will recount school experiences much as they would have spoken about other children they played with at nursery school or in the local playground.

I have found that some of these "difficult" 5–10-year-olds (I repeat, some, not all!) seen in the consulting room will eventually manage to explain their silence by voicing their belief that there is no point in speaking to the parents, because they do not really want to know or else will never agree with whatever the child says. Seeing children of this age group together with their parents, quite often we find that one or both parents tend to respond to the child's words with explanations, corrections, or instructions, rather than with any true interest to learn of the child's thoughts and feelings, whether these are logical or illogical, fair or unfair, right or wrong. But this finding cannot be applied to all children of this age. It seems to be typical of this developmental phase that the child becomes more self-conscious, more guarded, less willing to be engaged in a conversation, irrespective of how the parents relate to him. This attitude of reserve may be linked to the child's growing exposure to other environments and the possibility that the resulting comparisons, conscious and unconscious, may lead the child to imagine that the parents expect total fidelity and obedience from him and not any questioning of the ways in which the family live.

CHAPTER ONE

The child's view of himself

I remember very clearly the day when a friend of my younger brother's, a boy then aged eight, came to our house. At one point, addressing our mother, he said with a rather sad voice, "My mother says I am stupid . . ." We laughed, and our mother tried to reassure him, taking great care not to say anything that, if reported, might offend the boy's mother. It happened that we kept in touch with that family and we saw that young boy turn into a senior, very competent professional. However, he never managed to shake off that view his mother had of him. In social situations he was shy and clumsy, he found it difficult to articulate his thoughts, there was a lack of self-confidence that was difficult to comprehend when one knew of his success as a professional and family man.

It should not be surprising that our developing sense of self is so influenced by the views that our loved ones have of us. This is true at any age, but particularly significant when we are considering an infant or young child. It is quite an amusing and illuminating experience to watch a parent (in fact, most people!) approach a baby, watch it lovingly, and, before too long, voice his appraisal of that baby. But if most adjectives describe the baby's appearance (lovely, gorgeous, healthy, etc.), quite often we hear words purporting to describe the infant's personality (happy, stiff, dreamy, friendly, angry, etc.). Is this important? Without doubt, such appraisals will influence how that person addresses the baby and, depending on the relationship to the baby and his parents, the degree of contact that this person feels able to have with the child. If only visitors, this has limited importance, but when we focus on the infant's parents and other adults that have extensive contact with the child, we have to consider the influence that the images they hold of the baby have on that child's developing notions of his nature and his abilities, his self.

> A patient in his mid-thirties recounted how, throughout his early child-hood, he was considered clumsy, unreliable, and accident-prone. He had vivid memories of being told off by his parents for repeated acci-dents when he got hurt and things were broken or damaged. He was nearly four years old when it was finally established that he was severely visually impaired. But while the spectacles he was made to wear corrected his vision, the parents remained anxious about his capa-city to move around, and many years later he still considered himself clumsy and incapable of dealing with delicate objects.

Another example of the influence that a parent's view of a child's nature can have on his development can be seen in the following case.

> A man in his forties consulted me over difficulties he was experiencing with his partner. She accused him of being too reserved; even if prepared to accept his claims of loving her, she could not understand his incapacity to let his feelings come to the surface. He was aware of having this problem, but he had never managed to overcome it. In the course of a session, he mentioned what he called "a memory": one day he was feeding at his mother's breast and his mother had fainted; he took this event as a symbol of what damage he could cause. I asked him if this was a true memory and he answered that no, it was his father who had told him at some point in his childhood of that episode, but this had still functioned as a warning throughout his life.

I am not saying that the child's image of himself is *exclusively* the result of how he is treated. In spite of the considerable progress achieved in the research of what constitute inborn elements of a person's personality, it remains a huge challenge to establish what of an individual's characteristics is congenital and what is the result of his upbringing. Presumably, environmental influences cannot *create* personality features; supposedly, they will reinforce or inhibit characteristics already present in the individual's inborn endowment. Furthermore, we have to consider the possibility that what we would describe as the environmental input is already, in itself, a response to some feature of the infant. Good sense, therefore, should lead us to assume that we are the result of the interaction between nature and nurture. Considering that most of us tend to believe that an inborn feature is judged immutable, while acquired characteristics are seen as amenable to change, it is important to bear in mind that it is not so easy to establish the precise origin of the feature being focused on.

When seeing a family in the consulting room this differentiation is an important issue, since parents will often blame themselves for features of their child that, clearly, contain an element of inborn physical pathology. The way they dealt with their child might have reinforced or magnified these elements, but the distinction between these two causative factors (nature or nurture) should be discussed with the parents. Quite often, professionals will disagree on their assessments of the degree of improvement that a particular treatment can offer a child. Personally, when deciding to recommend that the child should have individual psychotherapy or some kind of joint family therapy, I try to discuss with the parents what areas of the child's problems may improve from the recommended therapy and which ones may remain unchanged. Such discussion should help the parents to reach a decision on how to proceed and also to understand how they can best contribute to the child's progress. In other words, in the same manner that the way in which parents see their child will influence the baby's developing sense of self, I believe that when they have a clearer understanding of a child's problems, the parents can also change the way they treat their child and, in this manner, help him to improve and overcome his difficulties.

During the first few years of life, the world of the child is virtually restricted to parents and siblings. These are continuously responding to the infant's sounds and movements, but presumably, from the infant's point of view, his perceptions will register how these others are addressing him and make the assumption that they are doing so in order to elicit particular reactions from him. We can find that the infant will remain (or become) silent when he is facing a person who is silent, while a smiling or singing person will probably elicit smiles or melodic sounds from the infant. The smiles, the gurgling or singing noises, much as the tensing up or crying, are all signs of the infants' unfolding physical and psychological abilities and of his establishing contact with the world around him. At the same time, these are experiences that leave memory traces, and they gradually enable the infant to build a picture of himself and of the world in which he lives.

We must always bear in mind that the infant's images of his experiences will most probably be very different from what we believe has happened. The best example of this is a situation that most of us have been through: making a gesture or a noise that we believe is loving and friendly, only to find that it provokes violent crying from the baby. Careful observation of the infant over a period of weeks will show that gradually the baby learns to link the image of a person with what he has come to expect from that person. Whether we admit it or not, the same is true for adults: we also build expectations of how the infant will react to each particular approach we make to him. And, unexpectedly, that day always arrives when we have a parent or a relative wanting to show off to us how well he knows his baby and proceeding to make a particular noise or movement to the baby, with colossal embarrassment resulting when, contrary to his expectations, the baby freezes up and begins to cry! It is amusing to see the parents' reaction to this type of unexpected crying: one of them will be surprised, intrigued, while the other will claim to know precisely what has made the baby cry.

This pattern, where parent and child learn what to expect from each other, can also be observed quite easily when focusing on older children and adults. It is quite striking how one parent will say to his child, "Please put that box down", in a tone of voice that shows very clearly that he expects to be obeyed, while another parent will say the same words with the intonation typical of someone who is convinced the child will ignore his/her words. It should not be surprising to find that the first child obeys the adult, while the second carries on as if nothing had been said to him. We tend to interpret these situations as demonstrating the child's firmness, weakness, obedience, defiance, and so on. But I believe that the child in the first example has learnt in the course of months, if not years (a) that his parent expects to be obeyed, (b) that the parent believes that he, the child, is able to carry out that action, and, finally, that (c) the child has a choice to obey or not that will lead to a response from that adult that has become predictable. This means that the child has learnt what abilities he is seen to possess and also the relationship between the adult's wishes/demands and his response. The situation is very different in the case of the second parent and child. Considering a number of such encounters, we find that if the child does not obey his parent's demand, sometimes the parent will react firmly, if not violently, while on other occasions the parent will simply give up and allow the child to "get away" with his disobedience. This means that the child is unable to predict which of these reactions will occur when he fails to obey the parent's demand. Every single case of this kind that I have met is presented as evidence of the child's attempt to "run the show", be in command, to be "manipulating", "controlling", etc. I think this is an unfair interpretation of the child's behaviour. My belief is that the unpredictability of the parent's reaction makes the child feel that the parent is not in full control of him/herself and this makes the child feel insecure, uncertain of the parent's ability to look after him. The refusal to obey becomes the child's attempt to test out the parent, in the hope that the parent will demonstrate his strength and, consequently, his capacity to be relied upon, thereby restoring the child's sense of security.

These situations are now described as the adults "setting limits", and complex discussions are held regarding the pros and cons of such attitudes. At one extreme are the parents who demand full and unquestioning obedience to their instructions; those who oppose this posture call them dictatorial, selfish people who ignore the child's rights and abilities. At the other end are the parents who claim to foster the child's sense of independence and creativity by not putting forward rules of any kind. My view is that, whatever else may be involved, it is beyond dispute that from birth the child fits in with his parents' way of life. Even if no explicit rules and demands are put forward, the child absorbs the parents' style of dealing with the innumerable details of daily life: closing the door to the bathroom or leaving it open when using it, moving round the house naked or covered up, eating only when sitting formally round the table or grabbing bites when hungry, the manner of addressing each other and people in general, smoking or taking drugs privately or in public, kissing each other when meeting or leaving the house, washing hands before eating or ignoring it—the list is endless. Do the parents demand that the child follows their example? Do they follow the old "do as I say, not as I do it" idea? Do they simply ignore what the child does or fails to do? The crucial point in all this debate must be: how does the child feel? What does he learn about the world he lives in?

I believe that for young children constancy and predictability are fundamental elements to fostering a sense of security. The under-five absorbs the parents' rules and expectations and develops a notion of routine that spells peace, a sense of what happens when and where. If rules are not clearly defined, the child develops a style of life that a stranger would describe as unpredictable, if not chaotic. When we meet the 5–10-year-old, we can see the difference between the children brought up in each of the above schemes. School and all other group activities are strictly bound to timetables and rules of behaviour. Children brought up with similar principles find it quite easy to fit in, since this new environment is no more than a continuation of home life. Sadly, the children who were allowed to follow their own impulses feel at a loss and repeatedly get into trouble when behaving at school as they behave at home. In other words, teaching children to obey and follow rules is, above all, helping them to fit in with the way in which our society expects us all to behave. Whatever other interpretations may be put forward, the central issue in this question of rules and discipline is the notion of respect for the others with whom one lives.

When seeing parents to discuss problems presented by their children, I have many times been struck by the way in which they express total bewilderment at the way in which the child behaves. "I just don't know where he gets this from!" is the typical cliché. Invariably, I make a point of explaining that I have no wish to find culprits, that it is pointless to identify whom to blame for the child's problems, that problems have to be resolved irrespective of who created them, but, after all these qualifications are taken into account, the fact remains that the child is born into a family and develops inside that same family. In other words, the child does not live in a vacuum, and if we want to understand a child's behaviour and feelings, we must take into account the environment in which that child lives. A lot of words! But a short way of making the same point tends to produce surprise in the parents: "Have you thought about the reason why your child speaks English?" Quite. Each child learns to speak the language that he discovers the parents understand; he learns to speak the language in which that particular parent addresses him. In families where each parent has a different mother tongue, the child will respond to how he is addressed: if each parent teaches and demands that the child converses with him/her in their specific mother tongue, the chances are that the child will indeed learn both languages and address each parent in the language that that parent speaks. Very often, we find parents addressing the child in English, while speaking to each other in another language. In these families, most children will learn and speak English (presumably the language of the country in which they live), but occasionally we find a child with an inborn ability to absorb and learn sounds who will also learn the language the parents use when they do not wish the children to understand what they are saying.

The 5–10-year-old who comes from a foreign family knows precisely what language to use, depending on where he finds himself. Meeting one of these children in the consulting room, I find that they will know to speak English to me, but if they want to voice a complaint to the parents, they will immediately use the parents' mother tongue, making sure that I do not understand what they are saying. I have never met a child from a foreign family who experienced any anxiety or self-doubt because of speaking at home a different language than English. Their sense of self contains the ability to adapt themselves to both environments and their respective languages.

CHAPTER TWO

The view of the world around him

The psychoanalytic theory of the development of the sense of self and other is intellectually appealing and, to me, very convincing. The theory goes that at birth and for a period of weeks the infant has no awareness of other human beings or of an external world in which he lives. During this period, supposedly, the infant would experience the feeding breast as an integral part of his self. At some point, the infant realizes that this breast is, in fact, not under his control, not a part of his self. A very interesting hypothesis is put forward at this point: at first, the infant believes the breast is a total, self-contained unit and only at a further stage of development does he realize that, in fact, the breast is a part of a whole individual, the mother, who not only feeds him, but also takes general care of him. These descriptive phases refer to the infant relating to a "part-object" and, later, to a "whole object". What makes this distinction so interesting is the fact that we find adults who see other people not as "whole individuals", that is, people with thoughts and feelings of their own, but only as sources that provide for the needs of that person. For example, a partner will be experienced as a source of sexual pleasure, but not recognized and treated as a separate human being with needs and sensitivities of their own; a waiter or a maid may be experienced as sources of food, but not as human beings who deserve the same consideration we give to those close to us. In these cases we speak of people relating to "part-objects" (some authors also describe these people as treating others as "need-satisfying objects") and not to "whole objects".

As he develops, the infant becomes aware that there is an other who, time and again, gets involved with him; presumably, initially he will not differentiate between different carers, but soon enough he learns to distinguish between these. A fascinating research finding (Macfarlane, 1975, pp. 103–117) showed that from the very first few days of life the baby differentiates between the smell of gauzes imbibed in the mother's milk and others that were used by other women. However, the recognition through sight comes a bit later. Gradually, the infant can recognize a wider number of people through using his vision and hearing. Other books in this series (Salo, Stoker, Davids, Hollins) have discussed the first five years of a child's life, and I will not go into details about these years here. They are probably the most fascinating years of a person's life. The baby coming to recognize each parent and those few other adults who spend time with him, then discovering and developing a relationship with older siblings and, in some families, with younger ones—observing these occasions can provide quite marvellous enjoyment when seeing the richness of a young child's reactions to the world. From my personal experience, a most magical situation occurs when a slightly older sibling tries to engage the baby. Quite often, as soon as the baby responds to the sibling's enticement, the older child moves away, as if losing interest. At times, before leaving, a push or a pinch is inflicted on the baby, but, even if making a noise to indicate he suffered pain, most babies go on to attempt to seduce back the older sibling! What can we make of this? Love? Forgiveness? A wish to pursue an initial experience of pleasure? An early indication of sociability? Presumably, a bit of each of these.

But, in the present volume, we are concentrating on the 5–10-year-old. Before getting to age five, most children will have attended a nursery school or, if not, certainly had the opportunity of playing with other children in parks or clubs or community centres. This is a widening of the child's horizons and it exposes him to contact with other children from varied backgrounds. But, in all these activities, the child will certainly have one or more adults monitoring his activities very closely. If the mother is not present, the chances are that the teachers or a nanny or some relative will be accompanying the child and dutifully reporting back to the parent how the child has coped with the hours when mother was not there. Even if child and mother are physically apart, both feel that emotionally they remain in close touch. However, when the child starts full-time primary school, there is a major change in the child's position. He is now away from home for longer intervals and not under one-to-one observation any more: both mother and child feel a widening of the emotional distance between them. In theoretical terms, there is a reduction of the relationship of dependence: the child has taken a step forward in his development towards independence and self-sufficiency.

From the child's point of view, this new phase can be felt as very threatening. Many children feel abandoned and try to cling to the parents. These are the children whose distress is openly displayed and parents should consider themselves lucky in that they know what problem they have to deal with. The majority of children tend to feel they must put on a brave face and try to cope with whatever difficulties they experience. Unfortunately, most of these find it easier to report good experiences and it is, therefore, always wise to inquire about difficult, unusual, or strange experiences, not to the point that the child believes that you expect these to happen, but rather to get across the point that you are interested to know "everything" the child has discovered, not only the "nice" stories.

A common misunderstanding can occur when the child mentions an event or asks a question that might be interpreted as an accusation or a complaint about the way things happen in the family. It is very common and quite understandable that the parent involved should respond by "setting the record straight": reminding the child of many situations that he is not taking into account or even turning to adjectives that depict the child as ungrateful, unfair, or even a liar. This is regrettable, and dangerous. Most times, the child is simply being moved by his sense of surprise at finding that not all families bring up their children in the same way. To quote a particular comment or formulate a question is his way of reporting his findings and hoping that the parent will help him to understand and accept these differences as part of normal life in society. If, however, the parent responds by reprimanding the child or simply correcting him, there is the danger that the child learns that such doubts or experiences must not be brought home.

An example might be the child who tells a parent that a boy at school was eating a bacon sandwich when he never eats those. Some common replies might be: (a) you know that Jews cannot eat bacon; (b) bacon is too fat and not good for you; (c) it happens that you are allergic to pork meat; (d) are you not getting enough food?; (e) well, perhaps you'll now make your own sandwiches; (f) did you ask him for a bite?; (g) did anything else happen at school besides your checking what the others eat? Once you consider how the child might react to each of these comments, would it make any difference if the parent, instead, asked (h) "and do you have any idea as to why it is that we don't give you bacon?"

I believe that this last question opens room for a conversation, while the others are an overt or covert way of closing the subject. And each type of response is likely to set up a pattern that can be very difficult to change. Five–ten-year-olds are very sensitive to what they believe is expected of them, even if it is often virtually impossible to pinpoint the moment where an experience led them to change their approach to a particular person. Putting this in different words, meeting a 5–10-year-old who is described as "shut-off", introverted, difficult to access, "impossible to know what he is thinking", it is not rare to discover that from *his* point of view, he finds it pointless to say things to his parents because "they don't want to know, anyway". Meeting such a child in the consulting room is a difficult challenge, since such personality features are applicable to many people of all ages and they can well be inborn characteristics, where the educational input *follows* such a way of communication, rather than causing it. Nevertheless, occasionally, we find situations where it can be quite convincing that the child has adapted to a parent–child relationship pattern where his views were not truly taken into account.

I was once having a meal with friends and, at one point, their seven-year-old son approached one of his parents with a request. Parents carried on talking with people round the table. The boy went off, only to return a few minutes later, when the same scene was repeated. After four or five such interchanges, the parents found it necessary to give me an apology: the boy was "just like that", he simply could not stop. Because these were good, intimate friends, I found it possible to voice my opinion: "But at no point did you really respond to him! I am surprised that it took him so long to give up trying!"

As it happens, when he became an adult, this was a young man generally considered as withdrawn and difficult to make contact with; meeting him now, how would anybody be able to establish to what extent his personality resulted from his inborn endowment or from his environmental input? And even when I witnessed the scene I described, how can we really be certain that it was the way his parents responded to him that led this boy to "give up on the world" and shut himself off?

When two people meet for the first time, it is unavoidable that their approach to each other is determined by their perceptions, and these are influenced by their preconceptions and general frame of mind at that particular moment. But, at each subsequent meeting, the memories of the first encounter will influence the approach that each participant displays to the other. Quite soon we have a definite pattern that will be self-perpetuating, since each one feels certain he *knows* how the other feels, thinks, and tends to react, and proceeds to address him precisely in the manner that brings forward the "predicted" feedback.

Focusing on the 5–10-year-old, this is a young person who has accumulated many experiences of meeting people of all ages and has gone through a very complex range of emotional reactions to these encounters. In an ordinary, stable family, it is obvious that home and family constitute the basis for his sense of security and continuity. Since the first five years of life unfold within a rather limited horizon, parents can feel quite confident in their conviction that they *know* their child. After age five, the average child acquires a growing sense of self-confidence and self-sufficiency that may well be related to the parents' experience that they no longer need to spend so much time and mental energy looking after their "little child". Starting primary school adds an external, physical dimension to this growing distance between child and parents.

This widening of the child's horizons is a normal developmental step. What is only implied in this description is the fact that the child's impulse to move away depends for its fulfilment on the parents' capacity to allow him to move away from them. It is uncommon, but not rare, to find "a clinging child", and this poses a complex problem to understand and resolve. How and when does this clinging start?

Turning back to the infant, when he experiences himself linked to a "whole mother" we speak of this pair as a self-contained unit. At this stage of his emotional development, the image of the mother is present at all times, hence the description of the baby being in a state of total dependence. Focusing on the mother, she seems to have phases in which she experiences the infant as a part of herself, a state of mind that Winnicott described as "primary maternal preoccupation" (Winnicott, 1956). Different women go through this type of union in varying degrees, and it is difficult to decide whether this particular emotional experience depends on personality or specific temporary life situations. Extreme examples would be a woman who has gone through long and painful struggles to conceive or a woman who has lost a child, and who then find a deep and powerful sense of "completion" and fulfilment when able to hold and relate to their infants. Sometimes they will try, consciously or unconsciously, to preserve that sense of union to the exclusion of other people. Outsiders may think it is "funny" to find a father who feels that the newborn baby has deprived him of the company of his wife, but the parents themselves have a very different experience of such situations. This close connection between mother and child is usually no more than a passing phase, but sometimes it can persist for months or years. When this happens, it will usually be recognized as a problem when the child reaches the point where he is expected to move away from mother and mix with peers but, instead, clings to her.

It is useful to discuss further the dynamics of the relationship between child and parents when he shows himself unable to move away from them. If the first five years of the child's life equip him to widen his world and move away from his parents, these are also years that pose continuous challenges to the parents, particularly the mother, who tends to be the parent who is more intimately involved with the child. Poets and artists have always depicted mother and baby as the prototypical image of a close, intimate relationship. But how long should this degree of closeness last? Many mothers have to return to work, some have more children or other relatives to look after, and, anyway, as the baby grows he will tend to move away from that elemental source of security. All these pressures of ordinary daily life will demand that the mother detaches herself from the baby and also allows him to move away from her. But there are times when some mothers find it difficult to make this step.

There are many reasons why a mother can find herself clinging to her child. The most common example is when the child suffered some serious illness early in life or comes from a difficult pregnancy or delivery. The fear of losing that loved offspring can be quite overwhelming, even if the mother is not consciously aware that this is the reason for her being over-anxious about anything bad happening to the child. A similar situation can occur when the mother has lost a previous child, as a miscarriage or a later death. But a mother who leads an isolated life, or who experiences distance or rejection from those close to her, can also turn to the child as a precious source of company and support. This configuration happens often in divorce cases, when both parents have to struggle to adapt to a new situation where the child will no longer be available to them at all times. As is well known, each parent asserts that the child prefers their company to being with the other parent, and any idea that the child actually prefers "the other" parent immediately leads to resentment, jealousy, and, sooner or later, hostility to the child.

By the time the child gets to the age of five, we assume that he has a clear and strong knowledge of those closer to him, plus the ability to gauge the characteristics of new people he meets. How does this happen? Presumably, what is involved is the child comparing one of more features of the new person with those characteristics of people he has met before. If the comparison is conscious, it will not be difficult to sort out any muddles that occur. For example, the child sees for the first time a colleague of one of his parents and runs away to his room: when asked for an explanation, he will say something like, "I don't like him, he looks just like that man who said horrible things to Daddy!". But if the child is unaware of the reason for the negative reaction, it may be more difficult to elicit the datum that triggered off that reaction of fear. Nevertheless, rather than simply ordering the child back or telling him off for his "rudeness", it is advisable to help him to find the words to explain his behaviour. What is at stake is not only the issue of politeness, the "correct" behaviour towards strangers, but also the child's realizing that his feelings are respected and that the parents want to foster his capacity to articulate his emotions, rather than just expressing them through his behaviour.

As already mentioned above, children have very different styles of approaching the people in their world. It is debatable to what extent this is constitutional or, alternatively, the result of their experiences in the family during their development. Some children go out to the park or to a new school or to a holiday resort and face people with a wide smile on their faces, while others keep their faces tight and the whole body tense, as if in preparation for some unpleasant experience. It is tempting to attribute this to the parents' usual attitudes to people, but often we find siblings displaying very different attitudes to strangers, even though presumably exposed to the same family ethos. But most parents and adults in general do not treat life as a scientific laboratory and, therefore, do not really stop to consider why each child displays whatever façade they present to the world; instead, we tend to come out with an adjective that translates our impression and, unfortunately, tends to make the child believe this is a true description of their nature. "My God, what makes you look so unhappy?"; "Wow! Have you swallowed some bitter pill?"; "Oh, good, have you thought of a good joke?"; "Are you thinking of what present Father Christmas will bring you?"; "Has someone done the dirty on you?"; "What's wrong? Have I done something wrong?"; "I guess you don't really like my hairstyle . . ." The variations are endless, but very seldom do such remarks really change the child's disposition. Probably the opposite happens, with the child feeling that his misgivings were justified.

Family views on people cannot but influence the child's approach to the world. When one or both parents have prejudices that are frequently voiced at home, these are bound to affect the way in which the child will react when meeting those particular people. All families will bring up their children in line with rules, principles, likes, and dislikes that obviously shape the child's beliefs and attitudes. And, needless to say, the way the parents treat each other and how they refer to members of the wider family are bound to influence the view the child forms, not only of the parents, but of all these people. Examples can be found in families with deep religious convictions that will often refer to non-religious people in derogatory terms and, much too common in our present multi-cultural communities, we have parents openly voicing their contempt for newcomers from other countries. Being over five, the child will clearly recognize the meaning of the adjectives from other areas of life and this is bound to influence his feelings when school or other places suddenly put him in front of that kind of person. Worse is when the child uses a word whose full meaning he does not really know and suddenly discovers he has offended the other person.

A more subtle factor influencing the views the 5–10-year-old has of the world in general results from the school he attends. In England, more so than in many other countries, the child's accent also tends to be seen as a relevant datum to evaluate his origins and position in life. Coming from a home where language and accent are simply taken for granted and considered as part and parcel of who he is, joining school and meeting children with a great variety of appearances and accents can lead some children to experience varying degrees of self-consciousness and suspicion. In practice, the school ethos is the decisive factor in this problem. The vast majority of children will react to new peers taking into account their personality and their social attitudes, rather than their colour, accent, or religion. If the school has the ability to consider its pupils as individuals rather than children carrying colour or religious characteristics, the chances are that the children will integrate very harmoniously. I believe this is an extraordinarily important challenge: to acknowledge and respect the colour, religion, accent, size, appearance of each child without allowing these attributes to become assets or setbacks influencing that child's position in the group.

In the past, it was actually considered quite normal that children should be taught from very early on that certain subjects and certain ways of speaking were normal and acceptable when at home, but that the world outside called for different standards. In an age dominated by the notion of political correctness, this is supposed to have gone out of fashion, but I suspect it is still quite prevalent in our society. Broadly speaking, we might consider that the under-five need not be made aware of these issues, since most of his life is spent at home or in the domestic-like environment of a nursery school, while the pre-adolescent over ten has reached the stage where he no longer obeys unquestioningly parental teachings and injunctions. This leaves the 5–10-year-old as the most sensitive age period for this question of how to reconcile the familiarity of life at home and all the pressures and expectations found in the outside world. On the whole, the average 5–10-year-old does tend to uphold his parents' teachings, but his peers are continuously challenging these principles and the child can find himself struggling to reconcile filial devotion and the wish to be accepted by his peers.

References

Macfarlane, A. (1975). Olfaction in the development of social preferences in the humanneonate. *CIBA Foundation Symposium, 33*: 103–117.

Winnicott, D. W. (1956). Primary maternal preoccupation. In: *Through Paediatrics to Psycho-Analysis*. London: Karnac, 1992.

CHAPTER THREE

Gender identity

I n common parlance, male and masculine are treated as signify-
ing the same thing and the same applies to female and feminine. These words aim to classify the sex to which the individual belongs. It is useful to establish a distinction between these
words. Male and female should be used to describe the anatomical
characteristics of the individual's body, while masculine and feminine are best reserved to describe the typical manner in which
people of each sex behaves. Using the word "gender" when referring to male and female makes it clearer that it is the anatomical
features of the person that are being addressed. Masculine and
feminine refer to the person's sexual posture, identity, and orientation. But in daily, ordinary life, it is the word "sex" that is used to
cover all these meanings. Considering that we want to discuss the
process whereby each child comes to grasp the details of his
anatomical characteristics and how he/she reaches the point of
seeing him/herself as masculine or feminine, I would like to keep
these categories apart from each other.

From a psychoanalytical perspective, the average five-year-old
is seen as a child who has reached the "resolution of the Oedipal
complex". Translated into non-theoretical language, this means a

child who has achieved the developmental stage where he experiences himself as a male like father, or a female like mother, and feels free to form relationships with other people in the outside world, that is, not bound by strong emotional ties to remain close to his parents. Of course, this awareness does not happen overnight; it is the result of multiple experiences in which the child learns about his/her anatomical characteristics and also recognizes similarities and differences between his/her ways of behaving and those of each of his/her parents. A little girl who enjoys combing her hair in front of the mirror will know this is a practice more often undertaken by mother than father, much as the boy who enjoys kicking a ball will know this is a game more enjoyed by father than by mother. But the fact is that, right from birth, the child will be treated as belonging to one particular gender: the clothes, the hairstyle, the multiple apparently meaningless ways in which we treat our child, expecting him/her to behave in line with being a boy or a girl. And then we have the endless admonitions, where parents point out "this is not how a boy behaves!" If there are older siblings, they will also deal with the child in line with the perceived gender, while the child will inevitably also see the siblings as models with whom to identify.

This process of developing gender identity is not exclusively a psychological one. There are complex and very important hormonal, anatomical, and neurological processes that influence this development. Some boys are born with genital organs that fail to develop outside the body and, instead, remain inside the abdominal cavity; we have children born with genital organs of both sexes, and many other abnormalities. These are, mercifully, very rare findings and pose specific problems that require expert help for both child and parents. In the present context, I would only stress the importance of seeking this professional help as early as possible. Denying the presence of a physical abnormality will, in the long term, benefit neither child nor parents. These are very painful, traumatic situations and, if at all possible, besides the medical investigations and the appropriate remediation, psychological support should also be offered to child and parents.

Even if the average five-year-old has already a very clear view of his gender, we can at times find doubts and even anxieties regarding his sexual identity. Hairstyle, types and colours of clothes, use of toilet equipment, kinds of sports that are practised—there are many details that different cultures, different families associate with the definition of masculinity or femininity. In most Western societies children of both genders are brought up in the same way, but, for example, a boy in a Jewish religious home will learn to keep his head covered, much as a girl in some Eastern families will learn that boys command preferential treatment. Presumably, from very early on, aged two or three, children can recognize that they are being treated as a *boy* or as a *girl*, but it is only gradually that they realize the significance of their anatomical constitution. The boy will urinate standing up "like daddy", while the girl will sit on the toilet seat "like mummy". The boy will have his hair cut short "as daddy", while the girl will have elaborate hairdos "as mummy". The boy will get footballs and games as birthday presents, while the girl will relish the new dolls. In countries speaking Latin languages, each child will learn which suffixes to use in line with the grammatical gender of many words describing objects and people in his/her life, including when referring to him/herself.

The challenge facing parents is that even if experiencing conflict over their sexuality, not many children are able to give them pointers to their emotional experience.

Dorothy, six years old, was seen for a consultation because she was masturbating herself compulsively. Hers was a sophisticated family of professionals, and Dorothy was the middle child, with two brothers, one older and one younger. A very intelligent and articulate child, doing extremely well at school and in her general social life, this habit was so totally out of character that it worried her parents. In the course of the consultation, the mother told me of a recent episode when Dorothy told her that she "also had a willy". Mother asked Dorothy to show her what she meant and was then able to tell her that what she was holding in her fingers was her clitoris, not a penis. The girl was quite resentful that her mother should tell me this, but my response was to laugh and say that Dorothy was probably trying to pull her clitoris to stretch it and make it as big as a penis.

Mother and Dorothy laughed at such an idea. Mother was surprised and amused, but Dorothy was clearly embarrassed, as if some secret had been revealed.

I was told a couple of weeks later that the masturbation had stopped.

Joining primary school and meeting a wider range of children, not only in the classroom, but also in the playground and in sport activities, will expose the five-year-old to comparisons with peers of both sexes. "Behaving like a big boy" or "being just like a girl" are comments that boys are bound to hear quite often, and the words of pride or reassurance that parents tend to use in these circumstances do not usually succeed in counter-balancing the peers' views. It is inevitable that comments made by teachers or peers have a very different impact on the children than the words of parents and relatives that the child has grown up with. Parents and relatives may comment in the child's hearing that this is a quiet, peaceful child, but if teachers suddenly challenge the child for being withdrawn or absent, this is bound to upset the child and make him question if there is anything wrong with him. If the family are happy that their son plays happily with his sisters and their girlfriends, but teachers voice their puzzlement (disapproval?) that the boy should gravitate to the side of the playground where the girls are playing their girlish games, it is more than likely that the boy will wonder if there is something wrong with his notion of which gender he belongs to.

It is important to remember that the child's behaviour is seldom the result of a conscious, deliberate analysis of how to tackle life. In principle, children will move in the world, whether at home or in society, in a spontaneous, unselfconscious way, simply responding to their impulses and what they have come to learn is the way in which they are treated by the people in their world. It is only when parents or others indicate their view that the child is doing something that is "not quite right" that the child will suddenly or gradually realize that there is a clash between his inclinations and the way in which he is expected to behave. What happens next will depend on how each family considers the behaviour in question: what attitude is taken will be the result of an appraisal that depends on complex factors. Supposing we have a five- or six-year-old who behaves in a manner that is typical of a child of the opposite gender: some parents may smile and consider this "cute", while somebody else may wonder about some hormonal or psychological abnormality that should be investigated. If the boy who wants to dress up as a girl is being brought up by a single mother it is inevitable (if regrettable) that people will jump to the conclusion that this is a mother who wanted a daughter in the first place. If the girl who behaves like a boy is the youngest of five daughters, people will easily brush this away as being the result of the parents wanting to have, at last, a son. Such behaviour can occur with any child and it makes a difference whether it is engaged in as a game, an occasional event, or whether it persists and the child shows signs that this display of features of the opposite gender is the result of a deliberate, conscious wish. In such a case, from a medical point of view, I see it as more prudent to consider a paediatric assessment before moving on to look at individual or family psychological factors. The medical and the psychological angles are not mutually exclusive and both of them should be considered.

We live in a world that looks at gender identity in a very different way to that which prevailed decades ago. Homosexuality is seen to depend on sexual orientation rather than involving any disturbance of gender identity. If, in the past, homosexuality was seen as pathological, now it is considered as normal and no more than a choice of what partners to associate with. Homosexual men were called "sissies" and some homosexual women might be called "butch", but these epithets have lost their impact, their implied meaning of some underlying pathology. When thinking of adults, these issues are given a degree of importance that is usually considered to result from personal prejudices, and perhaps this is not so relevant as far as a particular individual is concerned, since being an adult he is (or should be) able and free to decide how to deal with the issue. The situation is very different when we consider our 5–10-year-old, since the child under consideration is, by definition, not an independent being. To discover that child's actual emotional experience of his/her position in life will demand careful, meticulous, and delicate assessment. It is possible that we find a child quite content with his apparently "abnormal" behaviour, but we may also find a child who is aware of the impact he/she is producing on those around him/her and is quite baffled by his/her feelings and choices of behaviour. Once anatomical and hormonal abnormalities are excluded, it is clear that this would be a child in need of help of the kind offered by psychotherapy.

CHAPTER FOUR

Siblings

From the parents' point of view, the five-year-old moving on to full-time school attendance can be felt as a liberating end of a phase, but others can experience this as a loss. Some parents feel now free to devote more time to the pursuit of their interests, but we do find others who feel they have lost their child and, not so rarely, we can find women who start feeling broody at this point.

Many years ago, I saw a forty-two-year-old woman who had become very depressed. Successful in her job and an active wife and mother, she was baffled by these depressive feelings, since she had always seen herself as optimistic and energetic. She felt loved by her husband and she was proud of what her four children were achieving in life. We discussed various aspects of her life and invariably she put forward answers that only reinforced the impression that it was difficult to understand the reason for the depth of her depression. Suddenly, the ages of her children struck me: the youngest was five years old and the difference in age between all the siblings was also five years. When I asked her if this was relevant, she burst out crying. In those days, it was totally unacceptable that a woman should embark on a pregnancy when over forty, and this woman had just seen her youngest son starting full-time school: she felt abandoned and condemned to a life of loneliness and purposelessness that she found unbearable.

Children growing up as an only child are likely to ask the parents at some point why this is so. At what age will the question arise? This probably depends not only on the various environments where other children are met, but also on the personality of the individual child. We do find children (mostly girls) who choose to name a doll as a sister without actually formulating the relevant question to the parents. And this is a difficult question for most parents to answer. "One is more than enough, thank you!"; "I fear I did not manage to get pregnant again"; "I lost a pregnancy and I didn't want to risk another loss"; "Your father (or mother) did not want any more children"; "the love I feel for you would not let me have another one": endless possibilities, but is any of them fully appropriate or convincing? This is clearly a question that does not leave much room for the truth while the child is young. If so, then when should the truth be told? Personally, I believe the truth is not what the child wants to learn. I would go further and say that no child, of whatever age, wants to learn the truth in this matter and that it is much better to tell the child whatever it is that you, the parent, feel comfortable with. Only in very special circumstances will we ever find out what the child made of your answer. Every single adult I have met who was an only child was able to tell me what explanation he/she had from their parents for not having more children. Would the parents confirm that this is what they said? Surely, at the end of the day, what matters is what the child made of the parent's words and what significance this acquired in that person's later life. Considering that it is beyond us to guess how our words will be heard, elaborated, and retained by the child, I believe that it is best to consult our own feelings in the matter and not feel obliged to "speak the truth" or to "say what is best for the child". The real reason for not having more children belongs to the parents and, if a child asks the question, I think it is best to explore what leads the child to raise the question and how he/she feels about being an only child.

My clinical experience with children, as much as with adults, has taught me that whatever a parent tells the child about the reason for their being an only child leads to complex feelings about that child's situation in life. Much as his name, the colour of his hair, his height, and endless other elements of the child's experience of life, being an only child can lead to fantasies woven by the child to make sense of his position in the family. If, besides the obvious fact of being an only child, the person has also been given some explanation of what caused the parents not to have another child, this information leads to quite unpredictable (conscious and unconscious) feelings about self and others. The age at which the child is given these explanations is probably significant, but it is difficult to guess what impact they will cause at any particular stage. Those people I have interviewed who had been told the reason for the absence of siblings seemed to have taken this information as a possible pointer to what might happen to them when they came to have children of their own. Very often, the parents' explanation was taken by them as a reflection of how they or their birth affected the parents. This interpretation would most probably be seen as wrong, if not absurd, by the parents if they learnt of it, but the child concerned can take on a sense of responsibility for what followed (and preceded) his birth, and the resulting feelings of guilt tend to interfere with that person's approach to life, particularly to members of the opposite sex and the subsequent problem of deciding on procreation.

In most families, by the time the child reaches the age of five, there is one (or more) sibling to accommodate. The five-year-old's reaction to the birth of a sibling is a fascinating subject. Girls tend to identify with the mother and will, often, run parallel pregnancies with their dolls. Boys tend to be more reserved in their reaction. They will touch the mother's abdomen and will agree to listen to the baby's heart or feel its movements inside the mother's abdomen, but on the whole they do not voice their thoughts, as girls tend to do. After accompanying the progress of the pregnancy, it is still difficult to predict how each child will react to the actual birth of the sibling.

When the circumstances of the second child's pregnancy and/or birth are problematic, the first child may struggle to comprehend his/her position in the family, particularly if mother requires hospitalization. Ideally, the father should spend more time with the child and attempt to comfort him/her. Again, truth has to be dressed up, bearing in mind the child's ability to understand what is happening. These are always very painful times, since the parents are so deeply involved in making sure that both mother and baby improve and reach a point where they can come home. Nevertheless, it is important to make time for the older sibling(s). Considering what our unconscious can construct on the basis of our feelings, it is worth stressing to the child(ren) that the emergency that hit mother and/or baby is a medical contingency, totally unpredictable and *nobody's fault*. Our brains are wired in such a manner that most of us tend to think *causally*, always seeking some factor that can be blamed for a mishap. In terms of siblings, the goal in the present context is to address the possibility of an older child blaming himself or the new arrival for the troubles that mother is suffering.

All being well, mother and baby return home and a complex process of adaptation gets started. The new baby embarks on the developmental steps already described, while the older sibling(s) do their best to preserve their position in the family. Five-year-olds have enough experience of life to know that here is a new competitor, but they are able to counterbalance these feelings of jealousy through (unconsciously) identifying with the parents and taking a maternal or paternal role *vis-à-vis* the baby. I mentioned earlier (p. 10) how a period of charming and heart-warming playing with the baby can be followed by a push or a pinch. Quite often this is "caught" by a parent, and it is important to teach the child that this behaviour is not acceptable, but never to ignore it or treat it as a sign of intemperate sadism. Even when they feel bitterly displaced in the parents' love, most 5–10-year-olds know that they are at no risk of being written off.

Why do 5–10-year-olds react so differently to the parental nursing of their younger sibling? Like all human beings, children are very sensitive to how they are treated, but they usually fail to take into account the degree to which this experience is influenced by how they feel about themselves. If the 5–10-year-old is going through a phase where he is unhappy with his performance at school, he will turn to the parents for some consolation, but this makes it more likely that he may interpret the parents' care of the baby as a criticism of his "failures" at school. The child over ten is better able to feel secure in his position in the family, but the 5–10-year-old is still struggling with the conflicts of moving out of parental dependence and the longing for the comforts of infantile dependency. The resulting jealousy is normal, and they should be allowed to express their feelings, but, at the same time, it is very important to teach the older child that babies are vulnerable creatures and that they should learn *acceptable* ways of dealing with their feelings of resentment or jealousy; the same message must be put forward if the physical protest is directed at the mother. In other words, the child is entitled to his feelings and these should be treated as normal and acceptable, but only when expressed in a manner that is in line with the ethos of that particular family.

My experience with students observing the interaction between mothers and their newborns has shown me that an all-important factor in the development of the siblings' relationship is the way in which the mother introduces the baby to the older child. Most over-fives (particularly the boys) will tend to move away and avoid coming too close to the place where mother is feeding the baby or bathing it. Girls will occasionally try to join the pair, but often behave in a manner that a mother may take as being competitive. Under-fives are much more likely to approach the pair, and they tend to try to copy the mother's movements. Clearly, the variations are endless, but what I ended up singling out as the most important investment for future family peace is the mother choosing some points in the nurturing routine where she can make the older child feel he/she has a definite place in the care of the baby. Holding the milk bottle, arranging the clothes round the breast-feeding baby, holding him in his/her arms, getting the child to discover what sounds or movements will elicit a happy response from the baby— these are all statements of trust in the child's capacity to overcome his feelings of displacement and jealousy and put forward contributions that are valued by both mother and baby.

As time goes on, it is important to preserve this posture of acknowledging that some objectionable behaviour has occurred and must not be repeated, while fostering positive contributions by enlisting the help of the older child in various tasks required by the baby's needs. Repeating myself, if an older child causes pain to the younger sibling, the parent must get the message across that this is not acceptable behaviour, not by trying to make the child feel like some violent thug, but still demanding that the child must find different ways of expressing his jealousy and the wish to make himself heard. "Instead of hitting your little brother, just learn to tell ME how you are feeling—remember that he did nothing against you", which implies the message that the parent knows that the resentment is truly held against the parent who gave birth to the baby.

Besides these occasional clashes, watching the older 5–10-year-old teaching the baby games, showing him pictures in books, holding him while watching television, correcting his pronunciation of words are all immensely rewarding moments, when parents can actually enjoy the result of their efforts.

"I love all my children just the same!" is the standard assertion made by all parents, but how many of their children will agree with this statement? Consulted privately, every child has a clear sense of which one is each parent's favourite child, and this can be found at whatever age the person is when asked the question. But all that parents can do about this is to make sure that their feelings remain private and that, to the best of their ability, they do try to show the same love to all children.

A final word in this chapter: when your two-three-year-old old cries and complains that the older sibling did something wrong, most parents will react quite automatically, lashing out at the 5–10-year-old. Please do remember that being younger is not synonymous with being innocent! I have seen plenty of little ones who enjoy getting the older sibling into trouble. It is important to teach the younger one that his accusation is taken seriously, but this means a thorough investigation of what happened, so that the children learn that the parent treats them both equally.

CHAPTER FIVE

The child at school

E ndless fascinating stories can be told about a child's first day at full-time school. It is a question of standing at the front gate and watching how parents bring the child all the way from home and then face that moment when they have to separate from the child and see him cross that threshold, that door leading to the new place where they have to brave the world without the parents, and they, the parent(s) will have to turn round and make their way home all on their own. Indeed, some parents have found equally traumatic the parting experience when their child started at nursery, but most of them still see the primary school setting as a totally new challenge and it can be very painful to see how upset some parents feel when the child leaves them to step into primary school premises. And what about the child? The extent to which the child's demeanour matches the mother's (visible or hidden!) feelings is quite surprising. Sensing that the parent is upset, some children become so frightened that they burst out crying and refuse to go into school and again it is striking to see the extent to which the parent's reaction to the tears influences the behaviour of the child. However paradoxical it might appear, if the parent succeeds in controlling his/her distress and insists that the child will have to go into school, with a voice that is firm and quiet, not loaded with anxiety, most children will hesitate, tense up, as if plucking up courage, and then move on from mother to teacher. But . . . for an anxious parent, this degree of self-control is not easy to muster.

In this situation, the ethos of the school has a strong influence on the march of events. If mother and child are left to their own resources, the chances are that they will go home and wait for the next day to undertake a new attempt. Some schools, however, do assign staff to help pupils and parents in that situation and this tends to lead to dramatic progress. Other schools will offer that child and parent the opportunity to come into school and gradually become acquainted with its geography and atmosphere. Even when this is unacceptable to mother and child, a member of staff will speak to them in such a way that they feel that their reaction is understandable and acceptable, not final nor pathological, and this does make it easier for a more successful attempt the next day. Presumably, in these circumstances, both child and parent feel that the child will be in good hands and this allows the child to move away from the parent.

Once attendance ceases to be a problem, school life takes on a rhythm that tends to proceed quite smoothly. Some families have to struggle with the question of transport, but this usually does not involve the children. Perhaps two comments are called for on the matter of taking the child to school. Depending on a variety of factors, some children walk to school alone or with an adult, other parents have to use public transport, and others have a car of their own which is used for this purpose. Whichever means is chosen, this journey constitutes a precious occasion to teach the child how to deal with the problems of ordinary life outside home. This is not a question of "teaching them manners", but rather a serious plunge into circumstances that will affect them throughout their life. Crossing roads, using a seat belt in the car, mixing with strangers of all ages, sizes, and colours met in public places, deciding when and how to voice particular thoughts and questions when in close proximity to strangers—these are issues that will involve the children for the rest of their lives. In discussions on how these instructions, injunctions, requests, or demands should be made, the issue of independence is brought on to the scene and flexibility and rigidity are always mentioned. I believe that, in the final analysis, each parent will only manage to address the child in his own personal style, and I think this is fine, because it is very important that the child should register that the parent is saying something not with anger or fear, but with full conviction that he/she considers the message is important and is being put forward not to be discussed, but simply obeyed. Of course, once (for example) the child has fastened the seat belt in the car, the parent can explain to him why this is important, but the explanation should *follow* the belt being fastened. Another example is the question of not stepping off the pavement before the green sign for pedestrians is showing. Those parents who tend to ignore these rules when on their own must remember to obey them when they are looking after their child; they should bear in mind that the "bad example" might be put into practice by a child who is not completely aware of all the dangers involved in these issues.

We adults like to have a situation explained before we actually comply with what is being requested or demanded, but I believe that children should be taught that we do treat them as intelligent, thinking human beings, but that life contains situations where an adult's (particularly a parent's) request or demand has to be obeyed, complied with, without fuss or delays. Obviously, if such an expectation is displayed over trivial and irrelevant issues, the child will learn that this is an adult who just wants to be obeyed, but whose demands need not be taken seriously, since all that adult wants is to be treated with this particular brand of "respect". Surely a wasteful, self-defeating exercise. But if this kind of firmness is put into practice only when serious matters are at stake, the child learns that when that parent demands unconditional obedience, it concerns something important, and the child does do as told. Conditions permitting, this is the point at which a proper explanation should take place.

Another issue to be mentioned in this question of transport is the fact that a few children are sensitive to some kinds of motion. This can lead them to feel sick; some children will announce how they feel, others will suddenly vomit without prior warning and, occasionally, we can find a child who asks the parent to slow down or to avoid making sudden turns. While the first two types are seen with sympathy, the latter type can provoke angry reactions from a parent who feels accused of bad driving. This is not a question of the child "trying to gain control" of the parent, but a physical problem that has to be dealt with. What is involved is a disturbance of the inner ear over which the child has no control. One solution would be to find an alternative type of transport, but if this is impossible, other strategies (e.g., the child sitting in a different place, driving more slowly, taking a different route) have to be tried out, until one is found that enables the child to travel without problems.

CHAPTER SIX

Problems with teachers

T here was a time when, as soon as the child went through the school gates, the parents were supposed to step back and leave it to the teachers to look after their child. As time went by, this has fortunately changed and parents are not only allowed, but expected to keep contact with the school staff. Of course, each school organizes this contact in different ways; from the once-a-term parents–teachers' meeting to an open-door policy. However, not all parents take advantage of this and some will rely on the notion that "no news is good news" as a justification to keep away from school. In the majority of cases, this is fine, but, if at all possible, parents should take a more active interest in how their child is getting on at school. I see this as very important because, with the number of children attending each school, there is a real possibility that some children will go totally unnoticed if they do not give cause for concern or if they are not particularly outstanding in some way. This may well not constitute a problem as long as *your* child is happily getting on with his work, but if he happens to be a quiet, self-effacing child, he may find it very difficult to voice any problem that suddenly confronts him.

This "quiet, self-effacing" child is found more commonly in the age bracket of the 5–10-year-olds. They do not want to appear weak, needy, or deficient in any form and will try and present a façade of happiness or, at least, contentment. Many of these children find it difficult to tell the parents that their teacher is making them unhappy or that they are having problems with other children. How can parents guess that something is going wrong with their child at school? Impossible. The only way to find out is by keeping close contact with the child and with the school staff. Sudden mood changes, signs of unhappiness before going to school or when coming back home should be pointers leading to a gentle, kind, but determined effort to get the child to put into words his feelings about life at school.

It can be quite a delicate problem when parents come to the conclusion that a particular teacher is not handling their child adequately. It is reasonable and appropriate that parents in this position should request a meeting with the headteacher. What follows will depend on the policy of that particular school. Ideally, a further meeting with both headteacher and class teacher must be aimed at, in the hope that both of them are made aware of the child's needs and find a reasonable solution: sometimes, the child has to be moved to another class, but ideally the teacher may come to realize that she has to change her approach to that child. For the parents simply to decide against these meetings and, instead, remove the child to another school should not be undertaken lightly. The child will lose the company of some other children who may be particularly valued by him, but, more importantly, he may have a sense of failure and / or feel guilty for causing such a drastic change.

CHAPTER SEVEN

Problems with peers

T his is perhaps the most difficult aspect of school life. The "typical" 5–10-year-old will not usually give a full report of school events, particularly when starting at a new school. When first joining primary school, the child is aware of plunging into a new world and comparisons with family life are inevitable. Sometimes, the experiences of nursery school make this transition easier, but now classes are bigger and adult supervision tends to be well below the ideal level. Whether the child goes to a local authority school or to a private one, the chances are that he will meet a much wider range of children, many of whom feel insecure and are keen to "score points" that might heighten self-esteem and produce some sense of good status and self-confidence. If your child happens to dislike confrontations and conflict, he may feel intimidated by these new encounters. Sadly, this spells trouble, because the children who go in for tormenting and "scoring points" promptly feel in a position of power, having discovered someone they can bully.

Considering the position of the parents, we have only two possibilities: the attacked child reports (in whatever manner) that he is unhappy at school or he says nothing about it. In the first case, most parents tend to set out to reassure the child, for example, "it's early days, give it a bit longer . . .", or "aren't you jumping to conclusions? Wait a bit more . . ."; in the second, the tendency is to "let sleeping dogs lie". With luck, these attitudes may be perfectly appropriate and effective. Indeed, by this age, parents will have become familiar with their child's style of facing people and life in general. But even with this baseline of knowledge, it is still important to explore in detail the child's actual experiences. What is at stake is the possibility of the child not feeling able to report whatever events have given rise to anxiety or fear or unhappiness. This is dangerous, because it leaves the child exposed to situations he dreads while feeling unsupported by those loved ones he always relies on. At this point, it is impossible to predict how the child proceeds. Some do, in fact, find resources that enable them to overcome their initial fears; others are perhaps approached and "adopted" by another child who manages to make them feel safe and secure. But if this does not happen, there is always the possibility that, with the continuation of these painful feelings, the child's unconscious takes over and finds a different route to express the increasing distress: quite commonly, this is the point at which physical problems appear on the scene. The child may complain of tummy aches, sleeping troubles, wetting himself, crying with no apparent motive, etc. I believe each child (and adult) has his own, private, typical way of "using" the body to express distress that he does not manage to overcome or to put into words to obtain the help he longs for—I call this *the language of distress*.

By the time the child has physical complaints that prevent him from attending school, we have a very complex situation. If parents decide the child is ill and requires medical attention, we find a further complication in that different doctors have different approaches to children's illnesses. Some will take the view that any physical symptom must be thoroughly investigated and we have the child accumulating further traumatic experiences, besides possibly forming the impression that something inside him, in his body, is abnormal. Only if all tests results are negative is the ghost laid and, one hopes, the child may be able to accept that there is nothing wrong in him. But then we have the possibility of another doctor who simply dismisses all symptoms by saying "they are only psychosomatic", meaning that there is no danger whatever of some actual physical illness, and implying that by "being psychosomatic" the child's distress does not deserve any special attention. Sadly, concomitant physical problems can be involved whatever the child's emotional problems. All things considered, it is certainly simpler and more effective to ensure that an atmosphere prevails where the child feels free to confide to the parents about any worries he is struggling with.

If the child does manage to report, for example, that another child is bullying him, the parents should take this up with the school authorities. Nowadays, besides the class teachers, many schools have special staff in charge of supervising the children at playtime and their degree of competence varies enormously. If at all possible, it is best to request a meeting with the headteacher, who can then decide how to proceed. At the same time, it is important to consider why the child is not managing to defend himself. Sometimes we find, to our great surprise, that the child is actually seeking the company of the very child who bullies him. Even when this is not the case, I have always been puzzled by the difficulty bullied children experience when it comes to reporting the bully. Indeed, there is fear of being punished for exposing the bully, but I have seen children who found it very difficult to cope with the idea that the bully might be punished, as if this was something unfair, that they did not deserve.

I usually recommend that parents introduce the children to self-defence training. Some parents do urge the children to "punch back", but if this is not part of the family ethos and the child has not been exposed to physical force at home, they find it virtually impossible to "punch back". In this, as with all situations, it is important to consider the setting in which the child grew up. If exposed to physical punishment at home, children will find it quite easy to use their muscles to defend themselves, but if this is an explicit or virtual taboo in the family, the child will be incapable of using his fists to defend himself.

Another type of bullying that occurs quite often is peers demanding or just taking away the child's food or other possessions. There are children who cannot defend themselves and end up not having food to eat for lunch, and then are frightened and/or ashamed to report this at home. On a practical level, it is most important to raise this with the headteacher and staff, since it is the school's responsibility to ensure that pupils respect each other. Within the family context, I would repeat my words above: parents have to try hard to convince the child that they are interested in hearing of what happens at school, whether these are good or bad experiences. Easier said than done! As the child grows older, the more sensitive they seem to become to gauging each parent's reactions to their words and actions. When a simple, straight, candid report of an ordinary experience is met with words of advice as to how this might be improved or just carried out differently, many children seem to experience these as words of disappointment, as if they had not met the parent's expectations. From the adult's point of view, this is illogical and quite nonsensical, and yet it is what many children feel and this leads them to be careful about further reports of events. In other words, before reassuring or advising the child, it is best to get him to enlarge on his initial account and to encourage him to voice his interpretation of the events reported.

When dealing with pubertal or adolescent children, we almost take it for granted that they will not report to the parents much of what people, places, and activities they are involved with. But this is not unusual with younger children, and our 5–10-year-olds show this puzzling brand of privacy from early on. Repeating once again what has already been said: sometimes, the child will take words of support, advice, or encouragement coming from the parents as a disguised form of criticism and fault-finding. When this happens, we have a few children who will voice their displeasure or disagreement with the parent's words, which enables the parent to clarify their views, but the majority of children will just clam up and keep their feelings to themselves. The only way of avoiding this is that when your comments lead to some gauche silence or a discreet exit from the scene, it is worth bringing the child back to the subject and seek to persuade him to put his feelings into words.

CHAPTER EIGHT

School phobia

When your 5–10-year-old refuses to go to school you have a very difficult challenge to cope with. Each child will put forward a different reason to justify his not wanting to go to school. Quite often, this decision is first presented as a physical complaint, and once you take the child's complaint at face value, this shifts the focus of the problem, since you may well decide to take him to the GP. As you well know, some GPs will take a careful history and this may bring to the surface the fact that your child's physical complaints are linked to his fear of going to school, but another GP may simply take a perfunctory history and promptly prescribe medication, if not proceeding to embark on sophisticated but unnecessary investigations.

If you have learnt in the past that your child tends to complain of physical problems whenever he experiences anxiety or faces some activity that he dislikes or fears, then it may be worth your while to delay the medical visit and, instead, try to discuss the situation with him in terms of school attendance. When I have held an extended discussion of such a problem with child and mother (or parents), what gradually emerges is that one of the parents (usually the mother) is worried about her child's complaints and, furthermore, feels that it is simply unkind, if not dangerous, to force the child to go to school when he is distressed. Curiously enough, when the child is seen on his own, what emerges is that the child is worried that his mother is struggling with some problem and that he feels he should make himself available to her, in order to help when required. In other words, it is not that the child literally does not want *to go* to school, but that he does not want *to leave* the home. This may sound far-fetched and over-simplified, particularly when an intelligent 5–10-year-old manages to justify his "phobia" by quoting people or events at school that he wishes to avoid.

Of course, it is important to take the child seriously, but it is worth trying to discuss whatever the child is putting forward. In most cases the child does not just put forward one, only one, reason. He will complain of the behaviour of a colleague or teacher and soon enough will complain, for example, of some tummy-ache or dizziness. Obviously, if the child is running a temperature or also having other manifestations that accompany whatever he is complaining of (vomiting, diarrhoea, cough, etc.) then there is no doubt that medical assistance is called for. If the complaint involves school life, then it is important to discuss it in detail and suggest taking the matter to school staff.

If the point is reached when the child's complaints do not seem to have the validity he attributes to them, it is useful to consider that, consciously or unconsciously, the child is testing you out, to find whether you truly want him to leave home and go to school or whether, for some reason, you feel inclined to want his company. In other words, if your 5–10-year-old matches what I described as a typical child of this age, it is worth "forcing" him to discuss his complaints in detail. The diagnosis of "school phobia" is usually employed to describe a child who refuses to leave home and go to school, but what I would call "a true school phobia" depicts a child in a state of terror, full of anxiety and fear of falling victim to something or somebody that, not knowing how or where it would come from, he pinpoints as located at the school. Indeed, there are times when this sense of dread is triggered off by some feature or event that the child can identify.

Chris, aged five, went into a panic attack when his mother was taking him to school. This happened when the mother wanted to board the bus which they took every day they went to the school. Chris refused to board the bus, a decision his mother had no other option but to accept. As the bus was moving away, his panic subsided gradually and he eventually managed to name what had triggered off the panic: on the side of the bus, an advert depicted an enormous snake and Chris was scared this snake would attack him.

When there is deadlock and the parents do not manage to make much headway, it is best to seek professional help.

Jimmy, eight years old, refused to go to school. The family's GP referred Jimmy and his parents to the local Child and Adolescent Psychiatric consultant. Considering his history of good attendance and exceptionally good academic results, it was difficult to accept or understand his phobic reaction. The parents tried persuasion, rewards, punishment, to no avail. When seen at the consultation, Jimmy proved to be a very articulate, intelligent boy, but he was at a loss to explain his school phobia. His parents were present in the room and they told me of their past history. All seemed perfectly "ordinary". Father was some years older than his wife, but this seemed to have been well accepted by mother and son.

Jimmy made some drawings and when we were discussing these, he mentioned his father's passion for his motorbike. Parents laughed at the way he spoke about this. Jimmy went on to mention that father's journeys had become somewhat restricted because of being given medical leave from work, since he was being investigated for a heart condition. Both parents froze up: they had not been aware that Jimmy knew about this. At this point, it was not difficult to imagine that Jimmy refused to attend school in order to stay home and keep father company, making sure that nothing bad happened to him. After further discussion, I suggested that father should take Jimmy to school on his motorbike and, to their surprise, this seemed to break the impasse.

As it happens, I saw Jimmy's mother some weeks later. Yes, Jimmy was now attending school normally, but she told me of a long history of illnesses affecting Jimmy and both his parents, which meant that they all dreaded physical illnesses and their possible consequences. They had tried to keep father's investigations from Jimmy in an attempt to spare him from any anxiety regarding his father's state of health. She confirmed their surprise that Jimmy had been aware of the intense anxiety that both parents felt over the father's state of health.

Perhaps this will seem an unwarranted generalization, but I do think that whenever a 5–10-year-old indicates that he is afraid of going to school, this should be treated as a request for help over some fear that the child is not managing to cope with. If delicate, tender probing enables the child to name what exactly causes that fear, the parent has a focus for further discussion. If the child cannot explain why he should be experiencing fear, the parent should try to persuade him to go to school, arguing that this will give him the opportunity of discovering what exactly is causing the fear. But I believe the child will be paying enormous attention not just to the words used by the parent, but also to the emotions underlying and colouring those words. If the child picks up the slightest tone of supplication, he is likely to interpret the parent's efforts as attempts to say the right words, but only as a disguise to cover up an under-lying wish that the child stays at home.

It is one of the puzzling elements of human nature to find that when one of the parents is ill, one child may be only too keen to leave home and go to school or whatever other place, while another sibling will do his best to remain at home and keep the parent company. Clearly, this is a personality trait and not age-related, but in the 5–10 age group this wish to stay home and comfort the parent quite often finds expression as a reluctance to attend school.

There is no doubt that every single parent of a school phobic child will swear to the fact that he/she is doing everything possi-ble to ensure the child goes to school. Yet, some cases will persist for a long time, until the right way is found to reach the source of the child's refusal to attend school. I was involved with one such case many years ago, which I describe below.

Anthony was nine years old. A shy but intelligent and gifted student, it seemed quite out of character that he should suddenly refuse to leave home and go to school. His father had been ill and the mother was having difficulties in her job. As father recovered, he was put in charge of taking Anthony to school. I had several meetings with Anthony, with his parents, and also with the three of them. The meetings appeared very fruitful, but no progress was being made. One day I saw Anthony with his father and, after some discussion, we came to focus on what strategies the father adopted to persuade Anthony to go to school. Suddenly Anthony said, teasingly, that his father resorted to singing. Father was clearly very embarrassed, but Anthony had a smile on his face that appeared to suggest a sense of triumph. I asked father to let me hear the songs he sang when urging Anthony to leave the house. Very reluctantly, he did sing them:

1. "Miss Otis regrets she's unable to lunch today . . ." [because she has shot her lover]—words of the butler on the phone in a song of Noel Coward's.

2. "Hello, Dolly! Well, hello Dolly! / It's so nice to see you back where you belong . . .": meaning, at home.

3.- "Movin', movin', movin' / though they're disapprovin', / keep those dogies movin', Rawhide, / . . . Waitin' at the end of my ride", from *Rawhide*" a TV Western serial much in vogue at that time.

It was quite extraordinary to see that it seemed that only at that point where father sang the songs to me did it hit him that these lyrics were a clear, explicit message that he never expected Anthony to comply and actually go to school!

Not long after this session Anthony did his end of year exams and he announced that he would attend school regularly from the beginning of the next academic year. He did.

CHAPTER NINE

Sphincter training problems

At what age are you supposed to toilet train your child? I have always found the discussions on this subject quite fascinating. Some experts will give parents a definite age at which to start training and others will try and reassure parents that they do not need to worry because the child will become dry and/or clean (controlling urination and defecation) when he is ready for it. Because of my speciality, I would only meet (as one of my children said) "the cases that went wrong". It is, therefore, possible that my views are influenced by this "distorted" experience, but I am convinced that before we can put forward recommendations about the child's toilet training, it is important to discover what this area of daily life means to each parent and, from a wider perspective, how they feel about the question of imposing rules on their children.

There are families where the child will be put on a potty or toilet seat (depending on the child's age) and he will not be allowed to leave until a motion is passed. Reason? These are usually parents who believe faeces are poisonous (of course, they do not use this word themselves, they mention it only when describing how their parents and grandparents dealt with this issue) and must be eliminated if healthy daily life is to be ensured. I have seen families where children were *regularly*, *daily*, given purgatives to ensure that the bowels did open every day. At the opposite extreme, I have met families where children were wetting their beds at least once every night while the parents dismissed this as not significant (however ashamed the child felt about it), simply shrugging their shoulders and saying "it's fine, he'll grow out of it".

I have seen families where each parent knew precisely the time of day or the point of their daily routine when their bowels would open, much as I have seen other families where, asked this question, parents just laughed and dismissed it as an irrelevant question—"God knows . . . whenever it happens . . ." I believe that when discussing the upbringing of a child, it is extremely important to obtain information about the various aspects of family life that characterize the environment in which the child is developing. Some cultures will teach that when eating the fork is held with the left hand and the knife with the right one, while others teach precisely the opposite: people hold the knife with the right hand to cut hard items of food, then put the knife down and pick up the fork to hold it with the right hand. To some cultures, it is totally unacceptable that the hands should be used to eat food, while others use the hands all the time, practically not touching knife or fork. Turning to another area, it is perfectly obvious that babies make noises and babble until gradually producing the sounds and eventually the words that characterize their parents' language. Children will gradually learn to associate the colour and shape of their clothes and the way their hair is arranged with their gender. They will also find that their sense of hunger gradually comes to match the family's routine of having lunch as the main meal or, instead, the evening meal. As for bedtime, we have precisely the same process: the time of going to bed and the routine procedures that precede it are totally dependent on the habits of each family.

If these observations are valid, surely, we can expect the same principles to apply to toilet training. Focusing on the infant, the maturation of his nervous system and, specifically, of the bladder and anal sphincters will gradually lead to increasing control of these. This can be observed by checking on the increasing length of the intervals between successive openings of these sphincters. At some point, the infant can be seen to present visible or audible clues to his "being ready" to urinate or defecate. Ideally, this is the moment when education, the environmental input, comes on to the scene. Putting the child on the potty or the toilet seat (adequately adapted for size) can mark the beginning of a smooth training. It is enormously important to treat this step as a normal development, part of daily, ordinary life. The recommended procedure is that the child should be praised for urinating or defecating into the potty, but no dramatic "song and dance" need be made of this. If at all possible, if the child still wets or soils himself, some supportive, dismissive comment like "Oh, dear! I'm sure next time you will wait until you get to the potty!" should be made. The objective is to get across to the child that we believe in his having the ability to control his sphincters. In other words, we are trying to avoid the child feeling that he has a disability or that he is disappointing the parents. Easier said than done! Some parents simply cannot muster this kind of equanimity, taking (consciously or unconsciously) the child's failure to comply as a sign of their shortcomings as parents. If this is the case, it is best to delegate the toilet training task to someone like a nanny or relative, coming back to the picture when the child has learnt to ask for the use of potty or toilet seat.

As will be obvious, by the time the child gets to be five years old, these body functions have fallen into a pattern that has a life of its own. Children who have mastered the functioning of their sphincters will, on the whole, take this as no more than another item in their ordinary, daily life. Curiously enough, we find children who will, unexpectedly, present sphincter disturbances in periods of increased emotional distress. It can happen that these children interpret the sphincter dysfunction as a sign of pathology, or proof that they have not matured in a trustworthy manner, as they had believed. With these children, it is important to get across to them that we consider these disturbances as accidents, no more than responses to the crisis they are living through; it might be worth mentioning that another child in the same situation might break down into tears or have nightmares. The challenge is to enable the child to articulate the underlying anxieties.

There are children, however, who do not manage to gain control of one or the other sphincter. Some of these children may well have some physical abnormality that requires investigation. As a rule, if a child is still incontinent at two and a half to three years old, a GP or paediatrician should be consulted to ensure that the relevant organs are normal. But by the time the child is five years old, the possibility of physical pathology ought to have been ruled out and, if the incontinence is persistent, it is virtually certain that the child is struggling with emotional problems.

> Juliet was seven years old. She was brought to see me because she was wetting herself during daytime, both at home and at school. For several years her mother had been suffering from the increasingly incapacitating symptoms of multiple sclerosis. Juliet did extremely well at school, excelling in artwork and demonstrating a sharp mind and command of language. We discussed school and family life in general, and then focused on her having lost control of her urinary sphincter. I came to ask Juliet how she explained that she had not lost control of her anal sphincter. "Oh, that's because wee is liquid and pooh is thicker!" she said, as if this should be obvious. But, I said, how come you don't wet your bed? It was quite magical to see the look of illumination on her face: this had not occurred to her and she could now recognize the obvious implication that there was nothing intrinsically wrong with her body.

> I was seeing Juliet together with her mother and I found myself unable to put into words the common link of muscular dysfunctions involved in the work of their bodies or to mention the fundamental difference between Juliet's body dysfunctions and her mother's increasing incapacitation. But I do believe that the way they looked at each other at this point showed that they could recognize the meaning of Juliet's enuresis—an identification based on love and sympathy.

> Juliet's mother commented on the inevitable implication that "the body has its own way . . . it has a brain of its own . . ."

> Two weeks later, the mother phoned to tell me that Juliet had stopped wetting herself.

Bedwetting children will sometimes sleep on, ignoring the wet sheets, while others will move out of the bed and sleep on the floor, and still others will change the bed linen in the middle of the night. Speaking to the parents, we find the same variation of views: some react with anger when "discovering" the wet sheets, while others dismiss it as not important. What is surprising is that, while voicing their disapproval or disappointment or implicit tolerance—whatever words are used for these views, we often find that they do not really believe the child has the ability to change. The parents dutifully speak words that are meant to express an expectation or demand that the child should stop bedwetting, while in fact not believing this will come about, and I would argue that this unspoken conviction is the message picked up by the child.

Seeing bedwetting children and their families in the consulting room, what I found is that we have two goals to achieve. One is helping the child to realize that there is no *real* damage to his body—and most children can realize (usually with great surprise) that *if* there were actual damage to their sphincters, they would be wetting themselves uncontrollably all through the day. The other objective is to help the parents to change their approach to the child, and this is usually achieved by the implementation of the classical wall chart. It is plainly disturbing to find parents who are totally unable to make use of the chart method, but this is not a case of laziness or disregard, but a result of their underlying conviction that there is something definitely wrong with the child and that, therefore, it is pointless to think of charts when the child is not equipped to gain sphincter control. If we turn this upside down, when parents are firm and consistent in their rating of the child's progress, the child absorbs the message that the parents believe he is normal and has the ability to achieve sphincter control. I do believe that it is this vote of confidence that leads the child to overcome the problem and not whatever reward is agreed on.

A simple and good way of charting progress is to draw a chart where each morning a plus is given when the child had a dry night and, when this does not happen, a blank is left on that day. The deal is that when the child achieves seven dry nights in a row, some present is given. This present is chosen before starting the chart, and on no account must the seven consecutive days deal be changed.

To make explicit a point that is implied in the above, in physically normal children, I believe bedwetting is not just a problem of the child, but the result of complex child–parents' interactions, hence my naming *two* goals in a therapeutic approach. However, occasionally we find families where the parents' personality or their circumstances do not allow for these goals to be pursued. When this happens, some helping programme must be found for the child, such as psychotherapy or cognitive behaviour therapy.

An unusual case I met was that of a seven-year-old with whom my usual approaches led nowhere. This was a single mother who struggled with many problems of her own and had quite an inflexible approach to the son. My attempts to work with the boy and help him gain some understanding of his body failed. I suddenly thought of using a different approach that might suit the abilities and needs of mother and son. I said that the boy was clearly behaving like a much younger child and he should, therefore, be treated as one. The boy froze, dreading what I might be going on to say, but the mother beamed, already agreeing with my appraisal. I said that each night that the boy wet his bed, the mother should proceed the following night to put him to sleep in nappies. The boy noticed that the mother was in total agreement with my suggestion and he shouted, "You cannot do this to me!", to which she calmly replied, "Of course I will. It's clearly the right thing to do!".

The remarkable finding is that from that day the boy stopped wetting his bed.

We have a totally different situation if a child is wetting or messing himself not only at night, but also during the day. A physical check-up is mandatory in such cases. Organic pathology must be excluded before any psychological approach is embarked upon. Once we have a paediatric report that there is no damage to the urinary and/or intestinal apparatus of the child, it is important to explore the child's conscious and unconscious feelings. I should add that this psychological intervention is equally useful if there is an organic problem, since the experience of being different to other children and the focus of endless critical comments is bound to affect the child's self-esteem and self-image. Seeing incontinent children who do not have any physical problem, it is not uncommon to find that, in spite of the doctor's reassurance, the child and/or the parents will continue to believe that there is a physical, unchangeable, uncontrollable damage to his urinary or digestive apparatus. However illogical this might seem, it is a possibility that has to be identified and discussed. These situations have to be explored in careful detail, because there is the possibility that the child may continue to wet or mess himself unless and until these anxieties are clarified and dealt with.

When we find a child who is retaining his stools, again it is important to exclude physical factors. In the majority of these cases that come to medical attention, the child is unable to empty his bowels after having gone through a period of very efficient sphincter control. Usually, most mothers will describe this situation as an ordinary case of constipation and, accordingly, institute a number of changes in the diet, hoping that this will help the child to achieve again normal functioning of his sphincter. More rarely we find children who are clearly not constipated but, instead, deliberately contracting their anal sphincter and preventing it from opening. It is important to investigate the totality of the child's life experience, since this may give us useful pointers to what may be the reason for the child's symptoms. Some of these children with retention of stools will avoid going into the bathroom and this may suggest that the child has made some conscious or unconscious idea about the toilet that frightens him. Exploring the unconscious thoughts of some of these children, I found that they had been overcome by a fear that they might fall into the toilet and go the same way as urine or stools that fall into it: that is, disappear forever. An interesting case was a young child who had misinterpreted his parents' word for his passing water into the toilet: they said "urine", but he heard "you are in".

Bowel function problems that do not respond to ordinary parental encouragement, reassurance, or even "bribing" in the form of rewards for proper performance, should be taken to a child psychiatrist, clinical psychologist, counsellor, or psychotherapist for specialized help. I believe that even when children behave as if they are messing themselves on purpose, this is a façade to save face and they should be taken to see a professional. I have never met a child who was proud of being mocked because of his smell. Some parents do resent such children, because they believe the child is being defiant: this is a mistake and the sooner the child's face-saving bluff is called, the better it is. Every child I have ever met who had problems with defecation was desperately keen to get rid of these and achieve normal bowel functioning.

CHAPTER TEN

The child in the community

S ometimes a 5–10-year-old's account of his experiences, whether at school or a park or even at a friend's house, can lead the parents to suspect that their child is "falling under the influence" of another child. At this age, pairing can occur quite often, with both boys and girls. Usually, this is no more than a meeting of minds, an association that can lead to many positive, fruitful experiences. Quite often, the child will report activities or thoughts shared with their companion, whether of the same sex or the opposite one, and this can make parents quite enjoy the emergence of abilities they might not have previously recognized. In the past, this happened quite often over playing games like chess, but nowadays the age of the computer and the mobile phone has led to children pairing up to play games or exchange messages. And yet, whether in the electronic world or simply in social spaces, at times there is a subtle line that is stepped over and causes parents to worry.

When the 5–10-year-old's reports suddenly suggest a sexual undertone, this can be initially amusing and enjoyable, but there can be a point where this implication leads to concern and opposition. This threshold is highly dependent on many factors. Perhaps the most important element in the picture is the general attitude that the child's family holds about sex. The parents' way of dealing with their own bodies and those of the children is bound to correspond to the manner in which they have discussed sexual issues with the children and, particularly, how to deal with the sexuality of other people. It is very likely that the 5–10-year-old's account of events that seem to involve a sexual element will be strongly influenced by what information he has received from his parents over these matters. The child's account is bound to raise a much more powerful sense of panic in a family that has never discussed sexual issues openly. However, whichever is the case, it makes a difference whether the other child comes from a family that is well known to the parents or, instead, is a stranger. The age and sex of the other child will also carry implications for the parents. If at all possible, it is advisable for the parents to control their initial impulse to an immediate reaction and, instead, try to get the child to give a detailed account of events and to clarify any points that the parents consider relevant.

In principle, an automatic demand for the relationship to cease can backfire and lead to the child keeping encounters hidden from the parents. If the parents' concern proves to be well founded, they should try to equip the child to recognize the implications of the events he or she has reported and, ideally, to move away from that relationship. It is always useful to find ways of getting the child to embark on some other activity that might represent an alternative source of interest that, one hopes, would make it easier for the child to move away from that undesirable contact. Music or language lessons, gymnastics, and swimming are some examples. A rule of thumb to follow in these situations is to avoid voicing open strong criticism of the peer or the relationship itself, since this can lead the child to take up what he may see as a defence of the peer against the parents' "attack".

A more serious situation arises when the child appears to be caught in a relationship where the peer is leading him to do things that are dangerous and/or reprehensible. Giving food or money away are frequent examples, but at times the child is led to steal things from other children or from home, or made to convey messages to other pupils or to teachers. More serious situations can occur, like taking packets to strangers or helping to steal things from shops. When the child gives the parents some cue to the existence of this dangerous situation, the parents must sigh with relief and gratitude, since quite often such dangerous activities only come to the parents' notice through third parties. Of course, it makes a difference whether your child is the victim or, instead, the leading party of these associations, but in either case this is a serious, delicate, and very difficult problem that calls for prompt action.

The first priority in these situations is to establish how best to help your child. No doubt the school has to deal with such activities taking place on its premises, but it is unlikely that the parents will be able to play much of a role in this aspect of the problem. You should make your protest, verbally or, even better, in writing, addressing the school and the local educational authority, but do reserve your energies to concentrate on helping your child. If the worrying liaison involves a neighbour or the child of a friend, or, in fact, a strange child, you may find yourself wondering whether to report events to the particular child's parents. Of course, this would be seen as logical and fair, but in real life, when this happens, there is the danger of the other parents "solving the problem" by claiming their child is innocent and that it is your child who is at fault. In other words, in practice, informing the other parents is usually a wasteful exercise: it is best to concentrate on your own child.

In broad terms, abuser and victim have very different problems. Some professionals will hypothesize that the victim complies with the abuse by unconsciously projecting on the other party his/her own abusing instincts. I believe this is a dangerous and unfair assumption. Even if conceivably plausible, this supposed collusion may result from a face-saving attempt to cope with the pain and humiliation of being put in an inferior position. If your child is the abused victim, it is important to find ways of helping him/her to deal with the feelings of weakness and failure to stand up against the exploitation by the peer. Just teaching lessons of how to deal with any similar situations is not enough; if he were able to use these lessons, the child would not have been caught in the situation in the first place. I believe that abusers try out their luck with many peers and for a child to give in to these endeavours probably indicates a sense of helplessness and isolation, a need to gain approval, and a deeper unconscious conflict over loyalties and duties, and this calls for a detailed and probably long-term programme of help usually offered by individual psychotherapy. Ideally, the parents should try to explore the reasons for their child not reporting to them what was going on, but this demands gentleness and subtlety, not severe admonitions or drastic punishment.

If, however, your child is the abuser, you have a more difficult problem to deal with. I take it for granted that if you are reading these lines you are not likely to think that "the apple never falls far from the tree". Instead, I imagine you would react to such news with "How can a child of mine do something like this? Surely, they are wrong to think this is the case!" But life does bring us nasty surprises and, once it is confirmed that your child behaved improperly, it is important to try and find out how he came to behave like that. It is quite possible that he might have acted under the influence of another child or adult. True or not, the child will need urgent help and it is worth insisting that he sees a counsellor or a psychotherapist; an adolescent in this situation would probably refuse to do this, but an under-ten is still quite likely to admit that he does need help. If it is established that your child has fallen prey to the pressures from an older child or an adult, this is likely to call for the intervention of law enforcing agencies (police or the Social Services).

A psychoanalytic detour is called for at this point. At first, the accounts of victim and perpetrator are dramatically different, no matter the nature or the timing of the abusing event. Looking more closely at their accounts, we can see the pain, humiliation, resentment, and hatred felt by the victim and the justifications, apparently aimed at explanation, exoneration of responsibility, and occasionally (not always!) apology of the abuser. But, going deeper in this investigation, we can find signs of a sense of power in the abuser, sometimes also pride and perhaps even relief at being in control and not in the position of the weaker party, as might have occurred to him earlier in his life. More puzzling in these deeper probings is to find the victim consciously or unconsciously harbouring unexpected feelings of gratification at being the one chosen by the abuser. At times, we also find the child imagining situations where the roles would be reversed and he would subject other children to the abuse he had suffered as victim. This is what the psychoanalytic concept of "reversal of roles" means, and it is more frequently found in ordinary life than we might want to believe. An ordinary sense of humanity and perhaps also a religious upbringing would lead to a clear decision never to cause on another person that degree of pain that you suffered, and yet, quite often, we find people taking on the position of inflicting on somebody else the kind of pain that originally was inflicted on them. The all-important point in this situation is whether this revenge takes place in the imagination or whether it is actually put into practice. Self-control is, therefore, a central feature in these interactions. From a broad perspective, we have to recognize that the abuser failed to control his aggressive impulses, but, not so rarely, we can find that the victim also failed to keep under proper surveillance the possible consequences of his words or actions.

I must take up a problem that has become the nightmare of many families: children making contact with strangers through online channels. As with innumerable other problems, this is one that many people believe has never existed before, or they will argue that "it was never as bad as it is now". Perhaps we have to consider two components in this issue: one is the child using equipment or facilities that are available to him, but supposedly to be used only by older persons. Here, we must remember that pornographic television programmes and magazines have existed for decades, much as there have always existed various other means through which adults sought contact with like-minded adults. The second element is the vulnerability of children to malicious or plainly criminal older children or adults. This, again, has always existed in society, where younger children had their feelings exploited by others. Innocence, immaturity, naivety have always been mentioned to explain the behaviour of these victimized children, but we can also find other feelings that must be taken into account, like a wish to be accepted, some sense of adventure and excitement, even plain curiosity. To embark on a helping programme, all of these feelings have to be considered.

The fact is that we now have very young children spending time on their computers exploring no end of things their parents might not approve of if they knew this was going on. And this is usually put forward as a problem that allows of no solution. I cannot forget a discussion a few years ago on the dangers of television programmes; all parents agreed on the need to supervise their children's use of television and then, rather meekly and reluctantly, all of them admitted how they failed in trying to implement their conviction. Except for one father who, quite unnoticed, had remained silent throughout the discussion. "No problem in my family" he said, quietly. "How then do you manage?" all the others asked in unison. "We don't have a television set."

But nowadays computers and mobile telephones have become part of every child's ordinary equipment for daily life. Total control of how they use this equipment is, in practice, impossible. There are now ways of blocking certain channels and parents should take advantage of this as soon as or, ideally before, some worrying experience occurs. When dealing with 5–10-year-olds, this tends to prove sufficient, but it is prudent to continue monitoring the child even after implementing these blocking techniques. On the whole, it is best to assume that all 5–10-year-olds are more knowledgeable and resourceful than we are prepared to credit.

Whether we like it or not, it is virtually impossible to exert complete control of what a child does with his/her computer, short of not allowing its use unless when monitored by an adult. I imagine that the only thing parents can do is to encourage the children to report on what use they make of going online and, if this is achieved, the parents have to discover the strategy that will ensure that the children continue to trust them and go on discussing their use of the computer. Easier said than done, certainly, but still worth trying.

CHAPTER ELEVEN

The wider family

M any tears have been shed on the actual or virtual disappearance of the wider family over these past few decades. People move to other cities or countries, divorce rates have increased, and new partnerships mark increased distance from the original family, social mobility brings about geographic and/or emotional distances between family members: these are only some of the reasons that have led many of our children to seldom or never meet grandparents or other relatives. Having grown up near most of my relatives, I feel this new situation constitutes a great loss for our children. Unfortunately, it is not easy to put into words what difference the present, new circumstances signify. The loss of a sense of belonging is clearly there, but it might be argued that this emotional experience is not exclusively achieved when growing up in a close family community or, for that matter, that not everyone growing in these ideal circumstances automatically feels he belongs there. A sense of knowing where one is coming from is another sentiment that can be achieved when one is constantly involved not only with the parents, but also with other relatives of different generations. Growing up in a wide family network can produce a sense of having some other trusted adult to turn to when one falls out with one's parents, but again it might be argued that neighbours or religious authorities or teachers or friends might be effective alternatives. A more subtle sense can exist that the parents have someone else behind them (that is not the other spouse) who can protect them when they feel unhappy, isolated, maltreated, or simply longing for a different loving haven. Again, it might be argued that alternative sources of support can exist outside the wider family. We might continue with argument and counter-argument, but, at the end of this balancing performance, it is probably certain that at least one point is incontrovertible: the adults have the right to discuss alternatives and reach their decision with regard to where they live, near or far from other members of the family, but our 5–10-year-old children are not given the choice.

I remember a six-year-old girl who did not speak English when she came to London. She had travelled with her parents and brother, leaving behind a very large family, where grandparents doted on her and no end of cousins were playtime companions. It became a favourite story in her family that, as she began to learn English, when playing in the local park she would approach other children and ask them, "Do you want to be my friend?" This was seen as an early sign of sociability and capacity to engage other children, but very probably this approach did not come entirely from self-confidence and self-sufficiency, but also from a sense of isolation and a wish to create a new circle of children of her age.

As I write, the UK, as many other countries in Europe (and some in other continents), is struggling with the problem of immigrants and this has become a heated political issue. However, there have always been similar waves of migration that lead to protests but also to the eventual settling down of the new migrants. It is impossible to predict how long the present crisis will take before the new arrivals become accepted members of the local communities. Within the context of our discussion, 5–10-year-olds are perhaps in a less painful situation than children older than them. Under-fives spend most of their time under the close protection of the parents, and those over ten have to contend with newly-met children who tend to be more challenging or bellicose and who are forever trying to score points in the eyes of their peers. Using unpleasant names to antagonize newcomers is common practice and adolescents and puberty children can find this period of accommodation quite daunting. In contrast, on the whole, 5–10-year-olds are less prejudiced and more able to ignore differences of colour or accent. It is possible that this is due to the fact that they are, themselves, going through a phase of life where the conscious and unconscious images of self are going through complex elaborations, and this perhaps enables them to face differences without the sense of threat that adolescents can feel in such circumstances.

Perhaps the main advantage of growing up within a wider family is the experience of learning the extent to which it is possible to witness the evidence of differences while continuously experiencing the strength of bonds of similarity and closeness. In practice, each set of uncle and aunt, with their children, the cousins, have their own characteristic pattern of jobs, roles, modes of intergenerational relating, the way in which each spouse treats the other, even probably the choice of words for ordinary, daily communications, and this cannot go unnoticed by each 5–10-year-old living with his own parents. But, however marked these differences can be, there is no doubt that the child is all the time aware that there is a degree of closeness, a deep shared code of ethics and manner of carrying out daily activities among the members of this wider family that clearly demarcates them from the other people in their community. Some religious communities manage to foster among their faithful the degree of closeness that is found in the kind of wider families that I have been focusing on, and this makes me wonder whether many of the people who turn to these religious fraternities are not, in fact, trying to make up for the absence of the wider family network whose protection they miss.

An interesting question is whether a child growing up in a close family unit absorbs the experience as an intrinsic part of his emotional development or whether this close community fulfils some inborn biological need of the child. Considering this question as a sociologist would allow for a simple answer: communities (social, political, lay, or religious) want to isolate themselves from "the others", and families tend to form units with a *pater familias*, a head authority who demands conformity to his beliefs from all his descendants; as the child grows up he absorbs this structure as the "normal" environment. But, focusing on an isolated individual, the answer seems to move in the direction of the existence of some deep (unconscious) need to belong to a group. As discussed earlier, up to age five it seems the child is content to play with neighbours, friends, or nursery school colleagues, as if all these belonged to some periphery that did not interfere with another central level of relationship where the child sees himself as a member of his nuclear family. After age five this seems to change, and the child often reports doubts and conflicts stemming from comparisons he now makes between the family styles and values he grew up with and those of other children met outside the home. Such reports or questions should not be interpreted as "early signs of rebellion", but, rather, as an indication that the child has reached a developmental stage where he is able to scrutinize alternatives, learn to discern differences, and, eventually, reach a considered decision about the way he wants to live: that is, where he belongs, of which community is he really a member.

I see here another example of the type of "confrontation" where the crucial lesson for the child is not necessarily the actual, spoken message given by the parent(s), but, rather, the demonstration of respect for the child's intellectual curiosity and the wish to foster his sense of judgement: a most wonderful way of helping the child to recognize the benefits of having such people in his world. Perhaps I should quote a text depicting, to my mind, this process: Aharon Applefeld, in his book, *The Story of a Life*, writes,

> Once a day I would go in to see him. He [his grandfather] would stroke my head, show me the letters in the book he was studying, and tell a short story, a fable, or a parable. Once he told me one that I could not understand. When he saw that I had not understood it, he said: "Not important, the main thing is to appreciate this morning." Even this was beyond my understanding. Nonetheless, it has remained with me to this day, like a pleasant riddle. Sometimes it seems to me that Grandfather didn't belong with us, but had come to visit from other regions: he was so different. [2006, p. 33]

In other words, if your 5–10-year-old reports his puzzlement at the way in which another child deals with some particular thing or activity, the important response is to get the child to discuss the values and implications of each approach. This can be a rich dialogue, and it is important that the parent should also present his arguments, but whether the child fully understands it or not, or whether he agrees with the parent or not, the main message we hope that the child takes away with him is (as Applefeld describes) that he is valued and that, whatever happens in future, he can hold on to the memory of a parent who was happy to treat him as a loved, valued, thinking human being.

Reference

Applefeld, A. (2006). *The Story of a Life*. Harmondsworth: Penguin.

CHAPTER TWELVE

Sleeping problems

I s there a "right time" for a 5–10-year-old to go to bed? The obvious answer is that each family puts their children to bed at the time that they consider the "right" one. Probably the one point on which there is general agreement is the notion that children need "at least eight hours of sleep". By the time the child gets to age five, the chances are that he has already developed a point where he usually finds himself getting sleepy after a full day of varied activities. What turns bedtime into a discussion issue is that sooner or later the over-five resents having to withdraw and leave parents (and any elder siblings) to enjoy further hours of waking life. This is the point at which parents need to muster huge amounts of patience and, one hopes, firmness.

Honesty demands that we adults recognize that the children's bedtime consults not only their biological needs, but also our wish to have some time for ourselves. When the child is three years old or younger, bedtime does not usually represent much of an issue. The child gets tired and wants a rest, and the chances are that their sphere of interests is not so demanding or attractive. Parents take them through the bedtime routine and put them to bed, tell them a story or have a chat; the children are content to put an end to the day. After about four years of age, the picture begins to change. The child feels more energetic and his interests become wider and his urge to explore the world is continuously increasing. A further complication can appear when the father only gets home late in the evening: the children obviously want to enjoy his company and this can turn into a problem if the father also wants to spend some time with the child, while the mother feels quite strongly that father's timetable should not lead to her child's routine being disrupted. Parents may clash and considerable control is required of both of them if the child is not to dissolve in tears, feeling guilty for having caused the parents to fight each other.

I do not believe in prescribing rules for bedtime, because parents' views on this matter vary so much. It is much kinder and more productive to act on one's convictions, since the child will get a clear message and proceed to obey it. However, for parents to put on some show of firmness when, in fact, they do not mind at all that the child is not yet asleep seems to be a waste of time and a bad lesson for the child. Some parents deal with bedtime as a non-issue and then, out of the blue, one evening decide that they should take a stronger attitude and just explode, demanding the child should stop playing up and stay in bed, with no further protests or requests. This usually leads children of whatever age to feel disconcerted and insecure, perceiving the parent as experiencing uncertainty and distress. Personally, I believe that this is what children feel when facing a distressed parent; it does not really make much difference whether this distress is overt or disguised, since children have very sharp antennae and they sense the parent's upset frame of mind, anyway.

The fundamental point in this issue of bedtime is that once parents have decided what time the child goes to bed and what steps have to be gone through in this bedtime process, then it is just vital that they demand full obedience to the routine leading up to falling asleep. Some children like being read to, and this usually leads to the time when they enjoy reading by themselves. The child's age is all-important here, since the younger ones like being read to or being told stories, while the older ones prefer the parent to be there when they go to bed, but otherwise are content with exchanging some comments on the events of the day. But I believe the parent has full rights to allow himself to engage the child in whatever activity he/she enjoys. However, whichever routine a parent chooses, it is most important that a time limit is accepted and acted upon. Sometimes a parent is enjoying the situation so much that he allows himself "a little bit longer", but this sets a bad example to the child, who may well claim equal rights to extend the pre-sleep chatter or story-reading.

Many children are brought for consultation on the basis of having "a sleep problem". Some of them are described as demanding to sleep on the parents' bed or, at least, in their bedroom; others are said to wake up every night and then to refuse to go back to their bed afterwards, claiming a fear of falling asleep again; the variations are endless, but the most common starting point of these crises is the reference to the child having a nightmare. Nothing moves a parent's heart more than the idea of their loved child having had a nightmare! But how does "having a nightmare" turn into a "sleeping problem"? What I learnt through seeing children in the context of their families is that by the time they come for help, it is no longer simply a problem of having a nightmare, but what the child and the parents developed into a predictable routine for most nights, if not every night.

Anthony was six years old when his mother brought him for a consultation. His mother had reached a point where she was afraid of losing control in her attempts to get Anthony to go to sleep. Every evening at around 8:30 p.m. she would put him to bed, stay with him some minutes, chatting or reading him some story, and then go downstairs to read, watch television, or talk to a friend. Before long, Anthony was downstairs, claiming he could not get to sleep or that he had fallen asleep and suddenly woken up with some fright—many excuses, but it meant her again going upstairs and trying to quieten him down or, at times, allowing him to stay downstairs for some minutes longer. But this was not all: even after falling asleep, Anthony would wake up at some point in the night and come to his mother's bed, pleading with her to allow him to stay there with her. Whatever attempts she made to persuade him to go to his own bed, she simply never succeeded.

Anthony's parents had divorced when he was just under four years of age. Mother had a good job, where her timetable enabled her to keep up with Anthony's needs. She had many friends, and her family lived quite nearby. Anthony had no problems at school and his sleeping was put forward as the only difficulty they struggled with.

I found Anthony a rather quiet boy, who had some difficulty in expanding on his activities or describing his feelings about school, family, or his neighbourhood. He was clearly very attached to his mother, but any reference to his father sounded rather bland and shallow. After many attempts to probe for any anxieties related to sleeping, I ended up with a rather pragmatic idea that the only way in which I might manage to help Anthony sleep in an independent manner was if I could obtain his mother's co-operation.

I put it to Anthony's mother that a vicious circle had been created and the only way of breaking it would be if she decided to do this, and managed to stick to her decision. I said it was possible that, deep down (meaning, unconsciously) Anthony might have formed the idea that she really did want him to keep her company. What he needed was for her to give him clear evidence that, however much she loved him, she really wanted his company only during daytime and that at night they should stay apart. She could see this made sense, but how to implement it?

I told her that, whether before her going to bed or after she was there, whenever Anthony came to her, quite irrespective of whatever excuses he made, she had to take him back to his bed and withdraw to where she had been before. She looked at me as if this sounded like a joke, since she had just told me how many hundreds of times she had tried it: what if he came back again? I repeated what I had said. I thought that the message she was giving him with her words did not work and she needed to give him that message through her actions. I believed he would eventually grasp that (1) she believed he could stay in his own bed and go to sleep on his own, and (2) she wanted him to respect her right to be on her own. She said she would try it, but her voice clearly showed her conviction that this would be a waste of time.

Anthony and his mother came to see me again two weeks later. She just could not stop laughing. One evening she had taken him back to his bed twenty-four times before he finally fell asleep. To her astonishment, the following evening she needed to take him back to bed only three times, and then, no more. No further problems since that evening, for the last ten days. An unusual consequence of this intervention was the number of mothers that Anthony's mother referred to my clinic . . .

My argument is that, supposedly, there is a first occasion when the child expresses a problem that is, so to say, entirely, exclusively his own. But, depending on how the parents deal with this situation, there appears the possibility that the child now values the parents' response and unconsciously comes to reproduce the original situation as a test of what response he will now obtain from the parents. If the same gratifying response comes about, I believe that a vicious circle is established and soon it becomes impossible to distinguish what is cause and what is effect, since each participant is responding to the other precisely in the manner that justifies further similar responses. Indeed, Anthony's mother denied that she ever "encouraged" her son to embark on the bedtime ritual that brought them to the consultation, but she recognized that her new response to the son broke the vicious circle they were caught up in. In other words, even if her words and behaviour had been meant to indicate to Anthony that she did not want him to get out of his bed, there was something in her tone of voice and in her actual response that led the boy to continue in his demanding behaviour; once he got the message that she would not budge, the circle was broken.

Michael was aged seven when brought for help over his nightmares and refusal to stay in his own bed. Michael had learning difficulties that made it difficult to probe for what might be the unconscious conflicts that gave rise to the nightmares, but a long discussion with the parents clarified that their involvement with Michael's siblings (one older and two younger) meant that Michael was allowed to stay awake a bit longer than the others and to be looked after by his father. Michael clearly valued this time and he became quite animated, trying to tell me how they enjoyed each other's company. However, his account suddenly revealed that his father had a compulsion to watch horror films and Michael's nightmares were intimately linked to the scenes he had been exposed to. The parents, who were both in my room with Michael, were clearly embarrassed at this "revelation" and they promptly realized what they needed to do.

Michael continued to present educational and behaviour problems, but his bedtime behaviour changed dramatically and he now slept through the nights.

Perhaps I should recount one of my most amusing experiences in this chapter of a child's life.

Peter was five years old and he was driving his parents out of their minds with his nightly panic attacks, screaming that there was a monster in the room that threatened to attack him. Peter's mother brought him to the consultation, together with an older brother, aged seven. I went through my routine of taking a family history, engaging Peter to learn of his views of himself, his family, and school life, then observing some drawings he made and, eventually, making some interpretations of Peter's communications and then giving some recommendations to Peter's mother.

They returned the following week, reporting no positive results. We went through a new exploration of Peter's feelings and new advice on how to proceed. When they returned two weeks later, they had radiant smiles and reported how delighted they were that the problem had been solved. I asked how it had happened. They told me that after the last visit they tried different stratagems to help Peter until his brother had an inspiration. Instead of staying in his own bed while mother tried to reassure Peter, he got out of his bed, called Peter's attention and then went over the window, opened it wide and made some aggressive gestures and shouted words of anger and exasperation, screaming at the monster to leave the room and let his brother sleep in peace. After a couple of minutes, he quietened down and said to Peter: "See, now you can sleep—the monster has gone away!" And that was the end of Peter's nightmares. He had slept normally since that day.

A final story, showing how bedtime can become a lovely moment of closeness and understanding:

At Julie's school, parents had to pay for school dinners and choose what the children were allowed to eat. Julie wanted ice cream, but her father thought she should have something more nutritious: an argument followed with Julie sulking and holding tears back. Getting back home, father found that mother had prepared a luxurious salad for dinner and decided that it was fair for Julie to have her ice cream. He phoned the school and asked the secretary to tell Julie and also inform the kitchen staff of his change of mind. Needless to say, Julie was jubilant. Bedtime came and Julie just could not fall asleep. She wanted a drink, she had to go to the loo, she needed company—and the time just ran on. Eventually, mother lost her temper and father asked her to let him take over the job. He started to speak quietly to Julie and then asked if it was possible that she had so much enjoyed her day that she did not want it to come to an end. Julie blushed, nodded in confirmation and gave him a kiss. After some minutes of hugging each other, father left and Julie fell asleep, peacefully.

CHAPTER THIRTEEN

Divorce

D oes it really matter how old is the child when parents divorce? The answer is a clear NO. We live in an age where campaigners argue that a child needs the care, not necessarily the presence, as father and mother, of the couple who conceived them. This is definitely not what life has taught me. Freud did not invent the Oedipus complex, and whoever first put forward Adam and Eve as prototypical figures of a parental couple, the fact is that all cultures throughout centuries retained this image of a man and a woman not only as bearers of children but also as the guardians who brought them up, ensuring that generations of human beings were perpetuated. However, human beings are subject to contradictory feelings and impulses that can lead them to form pairings of the same sex and also to consider that the pairing that led to the birth of a child does not bind them to each other forever. What about the feelings of the child caught up in these fluctuations of the parents' impulses?

Religious couples may resign themselves to staying on in a marriage that they no longer believe is viable, and similar principles are followed by many non-religious couples. For many decades now there has been an increase in the number of broken marriages and of couples who conceive children in the context of relationships that neither of them believes is a long-term proposition. This has led to an increase in the number of single-parent families and much research is still being conducted to study how these circumstances affect the long-term emotional development of the children involved.

In principle, I believe adults should have the right to end a marriage that represents no more than endless conflicts and unhappiness. To argue, as many people do, that the marriage should stay intact "for the sake of the children" may well represent a true picture of that person's convictions, but this is, to a large extent, a type of self-deception. In practice, children of any age suffer greatly from witnessing the clashes between their unhappy parents. If life allowed for laboratory experiments, what would be found if children of the same unhappy couple were examined for long periods (a) if the parents divorced, and (b) if they stayed together? Would the latter option really show us children who were less unhappy than what we would find if the parents had split up? I doubt it. But I must confess to my cynical belief that some researcher might produce statistics to prove that I am wrong, that is, that higher levels of distress and disruption of life are found among one of these groups of children. This is the rather common problem with statistical research. Sadly, these figures do not take into account what each individual truly feels; he can only describe his personal experience of what life has dealt him. Even when trying to imagine what would have happened *if* his parents had chosen a different course of life, he cannot really go through his life again.

Seeing an adult who reports difficulties in social and sexual relationships, it is quite tempting to attribute the person's troubles to the fact that his parents divorced when he was very young. But I have also met many adults who blamed their social and sexual problems on their living throughout childhood and adolescence in a family where the parents were continuously fighting with each other. It is well known that we can also find people with emotional difficulties who come from families where the parents had a very harmonious and happy life-long relationship. In short, what we are forced to admit is that it is easier to build explanatory hypotheses when trying to make sense of a person's *past* life than it is to predict how an individual will develop in the course of his life.

Parents who are continuously caught up in clashes, whether these are loud and visible or whether they are restricted to moments of privacy, are exposing their children to traumatic experiences. However much a couple believe they are presenting a façade of harmony to their children, the chances are that the children sense that there is conflict between them. Indeed, some children manage to adapt to these circumstances and achieve a reasonably normal development, but parents are entitled to question the price they are paying in order to keep the marriage intact.

Divorce will cause distress and, quite probably, long-term problems for the children, whatever their age when the parents split up. In a discussion on the issue of divorce, it is important to separate out the needs of the parents and those of the children. The one point in this matter that is obviously unfair is the fact that children do not have much power in the decision-making process. I have met adolescents who suggested or even urged their parents to divorce, but no child under ten would ever consider this option. Late adolescents tend to cope reasonably well with life after the divorce of their parents. But mid-adolescents and younger children find this immensely disturbing and painful. There is no such thing as a "clean" divorce, but some are messier than others and the child is left to cope with whatever comes his way.

Ideally, a divorcing couple would be able to retain some degree of friendship that might make the child's life less traumatic. Ordinary good sense and plain human respect would be helpful. Indeed, all couples know this is the case, but in the vast majority of cases, all these qualities are thrown out of the window and one or both parties embark on an irrational battle where no victors are possible. And the child is left to suffer in these battles.

These are problematic situations that require outside expert help. A psychotherapist or a marital therapist or counsellor should be approached, rather than cling to the hope that "time will solve it", that the child will find his way of accommodating to the new relationship between the parents. Perhaps some examples will illustrate what is involved.

Boris, nine years old, was seen because he was having trouble falling asleep, frequently broke down crying, and, most unusually, had occasional episodes of wetting himself. The parents had decided to separate and father had moved to a separate house. Now, several months later, they were applying for a divorce. Supposedly, the parents had continued to have a friendly relationship, but, in fact, the only contact they had with each other occurred when father came to pick up Boris and his younger brother at weekends. Monday mornings he took the children to school and no further contact took place with the wife until the following weekend. I saw Boris and both parents together. They told me of their past and present positions in life and also of their views of Boris's development. It was very difficult to get Boris to speak to me and both parents told me this is exactly what happened when they tried to engage him.

I asked to see Boris on his own. He told me of his difficulties at school and his general unhappiness with life. He found it very difficult to talk about his parents and I invited him to draw. He drew a vertical line in the middle of the page and eventually drew himself holding a telephone at the bottom of this dividing line—each side was meant to depict the home of each parent and he eventually explained that when he was with one parent, he worried all the time about how the other parent was feeling, hence using the phone to speak to that absent parent. I said that he did not feel able to be happy or enjoy being with either parent, forever worrying about how the other parent was feeling. He nodded and tears were now flowing from his eyes.

After a further few meetings, it became obvious that, in spite of their continued personal, individual analyses, neither parent was able or prepared to move from their present positions and I urged them, therefore, to get Boris to see a child psychotherapist.

I first saw Mrs T when her twin sons were three years old. The parents had divorced ten months earlier. I did not meet the twins at that point. She told me of her relationship with the father of the twins, and it was quite disturbing to hear how two sophisticated, middle-class professionals were able to torment each other in such crude manner. On one occasion, father came to the house to see the boys and, when Mrs T refused to let him in, he started banging so violently at the door that Mrs T called the police. Both children were crying in a state of fear.

It was four years later that Mrs T consulted me again because both boys were experiencing considerable difficulties in their home and school life. One of them had developed sleeping problems, often waking up in inconsolable tears, while the other had become increasingly withdrawn and also presenting difficulties with finding words to express himself. Mrs T had now found a new partner, but father remained unpredictable in his approach to the children. She also told me that there had been no change in the way in which she and the father of the boys treated each other and clashes between them occurred virtually every week. When I saw the boys, they came across as normally developing boys, one of them perhaps showing mannerisms that would usually be associated with a girl. More significantly, they were completely unable to say anything about the relationship between the parents. I thought that only continued, regular interviews with a professional might lead to each boy feeling sufficiently secure to bring himself to put into words the feelings that underlay their emotional and behaviour difficulties.

I saw the mother again on her own to discuss my impressions of the situation. She told me that she and her husband had not reached an agreement to see a marriage counsellor, so that both parents were seeing individual therapists, but I could not believe that they would achieve significant changes in the short-term, while I felt the children needed urgent professional help. I urged her, therefore, to consider individual therapy for both children.

I should explain the rationale for my recommendations. The two accounts above make it clear that I felt these were boys who were experiencing considerable emotional tension and suffering. Pathology? My impression was that it was the two sets of parents who needed to change their behaviour and it was painful to find that even though all four of them were going through some kind of psychotherapy, they seemed quite incapable of implementing significant changes in their manner of treating each other that might reduce the suffering of their children. So, why did I suggest that the children saw an analyst or therapist? Definitely not to relieve them of any pathology, but rather to give them the opportunity of finding a sympathetic person who would enable them to put their innermost feelings into words, without criticism or any type of pressure, let alone giving them facile advice on how to behave. To my mind, these children did not need to be told that their sleeping problems or enuresis were their way of expressing the distress they were experiencing in their lives. In my experience, being able to articulate or to hear the words that acknowledge the emotional impact that life circumstances are producing on them is enough to make the "symptoms" disappear. But most of our children do not have close adults other than their parents that they can turn to and voice their pain, hence the recommendation that professional help was required.

Divorce may be less traumatic for those children who have access to other family members. It should be mandatory that divorcing parents continue to allow the children to have contact with members of the families of both of them. This gives the children a sense of continuity and also the opportunity of meeting each parent together with the other members of their respective families.

Considering children in our age group, the 5–10-year-olds, their personalities must be taken into account and respected if parents decide on a divorce. Under-fives are more likely to express their despair in an open way and also to ask those questions that parents tend to find very difficult to answer. Over tens will usually try hard not to take sides and concentrate on practical questions regarding the arrangements that each parent will make for their future life. But 5–10-year-olds usually react with a sense of helplessness and disbelief, not quite able to figure out what shape life will take once the parents split up. Direct questions are not frequent, and this, paradoxically, makes it more difficult for the parents to explain their positions or to know what reassurance to offer the children regarding future patterns of life. In the above example, Boris had a younger brother, aged six, and he was described by the parents as behaving in a quiet, obedient, self-effacing way, as if quite content with whatever arrangements the parents made to organize contact with the father. How can we measure the amount of distress experienced by each sibling? Because of his physical symptoms Boris found his way to a psychotherapist, but are we being neglectful when not undertaking a similar step to enable his brother to voice his feelings? Is this a regrettable posture of "letting sleeping dogs lie", or is it, in practice, best to give the boy time to elaborate his feelings? Of course, each parent and each professional will make their own decision in such situations. Only time can tell whether the right course of action was taken.

CHAPTER FOURTEEN

Adoption

I t is possible that not many readers expected to find this chapter in this book, and perhaps an explanation is called for.

I once saw Robert, a seven-year-old, who was presenting behaviour problems at school and also wetting his bed. His mother brought him to the consultation, together with two younger siblings, aged two and four. Mother explained that she had been unable to conceive and decided to adopt Robert. To her surprise, she found herself conceiving the two other children. But, as our consultation proceeded, she kept referring to Robert as adopted, until he suddenly broke down crying and said, "Do you really have to go on saying it so many times?"

I saw this episode as a dramatic and painful demonstration of how complex it is to gauge the issue of acceptance. Whatever led the mother to keep reminding me of Robert's origins, the boy's reaction demonstrated his struggles to see himself as no more than another one of her children, rather than someone whose origins had to be spelt out each time an opportunity arose.

For many decades now, the recommended policy in the matter of adoption has been that the child must be told the truth of his position in the family *"as soon as he is ready for this"*. But how do parents decide that the child is ready to learn of his true origin? Do they consult the child's wishes, or do they rely on their own judgement?

There was a time when many papers were published in the psychoanalytic world taking up a favourite theme of books and legends: the child's fantasies of not being a real child of his parents, but in truth having been born to a royal family and no more than adopted by the present, "ordinary" parents. It is conceivable that if a child feels loved and secure in his family, he can afford to fantasize having a noble origin. Equally possible would be the opposite situation, where the child's resentment against one or both parents leads him to the comforting imagining that, in truth, he belongs to a higher level of society. These fantasies are very common and, whatever the feelings that lead to their existence, the child will always *know* that these thoughts are make-believe stories. Which means that the fantasies do not create doubts that might lead them to question the parents whether they are their real, biological parents. Nevertheless, we do find children who will ask the parents whether they are their "real" parents, usually a good opportunity to have some fun exploring what is behind the question. (I was seven years old when one day I asked my father what made him sometimes speak to my mother about "our son", and other times refer to me as "your [my mother's] son".) In these situations, it may be safe to assume that the question is only being formulated because the child is fairly certain that these are his real parents. When, instead, the child is actually suspicious that he was not informed of his true relationship with the parents, this should become apparent in the manner that the question is raised and it is very important that the parents explore how the question arose. The chances are that the child has heard some comment that gave rise to these anxieties and, in such a case, the parents should feel proud of being asked the question, since this kind of question is only asked when the child feels secure enough in the parents' love. And this gives them the chance to clarify the situation.

The age at which a child is adopted constitutes a fundamental, qualitative factor that must be taken into account when considering the child's emotional development and the role played by the adoptive parents in the child's life. When a child is adopted soon after birth or at a very early stage of life, by the time he becomes able to discern the difference between self and other (see earlier chapter) it is the adoptive parents who are registered as the nearest care-taking, nurturing people in that child's life. I do not believe that detailed observation, however close, of an infant and his parents would ever succeed in eliciting any datum in the infant's behaviour that might constitute evidence of his being adopted, rather than being given birth by that mother.

The same would never apply to the parents. Adopting an infant or a young child is an enormously complex challenge for any cou-ple. They have to adapt to a new situation, presumably after years of struggle trying to reach and then implement decisions and cope with frustrations: first, trying to have a child of their own, then the discovery that this is not possible, then to consider resigning them-selves to having no children or to adopt one, then months or years of administrative, technical steps and fruitless searches, etc. By the time they have an actual child in their hands, this cannot but repre-sent a revolution in their lives. Much as biological parents, they can only deal with the *present*, since it is impossible to predict what the future holds. And it is not surprising that a child's development brings endless moments of joy and gratification, but also plenty of frustration, anxiety, and pain. And we can take it for granted that biological parents and adoptive parents do not experience these moments in the same manner.

I am trying to emphasize the point that adoption is a complex problem, but not only for the child. It is equally important to consider how it affects the adopting parents. When the question arises "how old should the child be when we tell him about adop-tion", we must also consider how far have the parents gone in the process of adaptation to their chosen role.

When parents adopt a child who had been in the care of an institution or of foster parents, they are taking over a child who must have gone through endless efforts to make sense of the world in which he is growing up. We must take it for granted that the child has lived through no end of comments and attitudes related to his position in the world. It is unlikely that the child would have had the opportunity of close, competent help to disentangle his interpretations of all the experiences he has accumulated. Life being what it is, the chances are that he has been given no end of "statements of fact", information put forward by workers with different levels of sensitivity to what reaction their words produce. Put in different words, this is a child with innumerable experiences at the hands of adults and other children. The new parents will be seen and heard against a complex background of images (conscious and unconscious) that the child has accumulated of how other adults treated him. Even if the adopting parents try hard to be loving, tolerating, accepting, they must be prepared to deal with attitudes of suspicion and insecurity, particularly when (depending on the child's age and personality) these feelings are displayed in ways that appear ungrateful, disrespectful, perhaps even offending. To achieve this degree of tolerance is, of course, a tremendous challenge. Adoptive parents are also human and they have their breaking point, like all of us. But I would suggest that, if at all possible, it is best not to use words purporting to show love, forgiveness, or reassurance: if the child can believe the sincerity of these words, it is superfluous to utter them, while if the child is not able to believe them, it is pointless to say them. The ideal solution would be for the parents to show that they can grasp and understand the feelings expressed by the child (of whatever age), but that they are not taking them personally; they remain determined to continue the task they have undertaken, to help that child to reach maturity, self-sufficiency, and independence. But this cannot be done in words alone; it will always be the parents' face, tone of voice, and general demeanour that will convey to the child how they feel about the child's words or behaviour.

Taking into account all the factors described above, a word about the 5–10-year-old. The only general point I feel able to make is that, in this age bracket, the child will probably behave as if taking life at face value. Those children adopted later than during infancy, that is, children who have a definite memory of having been looked after by other adults than the adoptive parents, may display challenging behaviour resulting from their insecurity, but they tend to be relatively easy to reassure and to accept that these present adults are determined to stick to them. When the child was adopted at infancy and grows up believing these are his biological parents, the chances are that he will develop as if not really adopted. Problems may arise if, at some point, somebody else makes a comment to them about their origin. If they approach the parents to question this, it is best to present the truth, but always trying to answer only the questions that the child asks and not to pour out endless stories that the child might, in fact, prefer not to know about. When it is the parents who decide to inform the child of his origins, it can only be hoped that they choose a point when the child is ready to cope with this information. Again, I would argue, it is important to gauge the child's ability and desire to discover the complete truth of his origins.

When adoption involves various social and health authorities, we can discover that, even if trying to implement legal procedures, workers cannot dispose completely of their personal prejudices. Parents cannot do much about these situations, but it is important to take them into account when aiming at getting a personal viewpoint across.

I saw Martine when she was seven years old. She was a charming but shy girl, whose teachers had become worried about her being "in a dream world of her own" for long periods, not responding to them with more than her typical sweet smile. Martine had been placed in a family with a view to her adoption, after having spent years under the care of her local council's Social Services, after her single mother was considered unable to look after her. The new family consisted of a widowed mother and her two sons, aged seventeen and fifteen.

Martine gradually managed to respond to my approaches and engaged in a game of "squiggles", where each of us would make a squiggle and the other would then use this as a starting point to compose whatever image they made of it. In the course of this game, she came to tell me of her life at home. This contained references to sexual games, and her words led me to formulate the impression that her older brothers were sexually abusing her. I asked her several questions to investigate this possibility, but her replies gave me no further elements to prove or disprove my impression.

I invited the prospective adopting mother to discuss my views and she repeatedly dismissed as unreliable and irrelevant whatever Martine might have said. From her point of view, her sons' behaviour was above suspicion and my anxiety was totally unfounded.

I called a meeting involving the Social Workers involved in the case and the Medical Officer responsible for the health of children in that borough. It turned out that one of the social workers had already suspected that abuse was taking place and they were hoping I could offer some evidence to reach an appropriate decision. I had to admit I was unable to do this, and what became clear is that the mother did not seem to offer any reassurance that she might be able and willing to look into the matter. In practice, this meant that Martine's placement seemed unreliable and that she would have to be removed from that family. Besides returning to the care of Social Services, Martine was offered a vacancy for individual psychotherapy.

There was, however, a further chapter to this story. The Medical Officer called on me after a few days and took me to task over my behaviour: surely, she argued, living in a family is just priceless, any family unit is better for a child than living in a Social Services home. She quoted the experience of children separated from their parents during the Second World War, but I could not accept that this was a valid argument regarding Martine's placement.

On the whole, the age group we are focusing on does not constitute the time when adopted children experience or present the most difficult problems. Their sense of dependence and the desire to be "on the right side" of the adoptive parents will create a conscious and unconscious need and wish to feel close to and accepted by the parents. It is usually only at puberty that the first steps to move away from the dependence on the parents will lead to challenges to the truth and reliability of the parents' love.

As a general rule of thumb, I would suggest that the main area of conflict for the adopting parents lies in that classical question that we ask so often when taken by surprise by a child's words or behaviour: "who does he take after?" This clearly means "how can I explain his behaving like that?" and, predictably, if we can identify *who* the child's behaviour is reminding us of, it is almost certain that we feel on familiar territory and a solution will usually come to mind. When, instead, we hit the realization that the child's behaviour probably originates in a person, place, or circumstances that are totally out of our knowledge, we are left with a soul-destroying sense of helplessness that is not helpful to any of the participants.

CHAPTER FIFTEEN

Absences

I have already referred several times in this book to societal changes that have affected our lives. Children are sent to holiday colonies while parents travel on holidays abroad; working in firms with international interests demands that one or both parents travel abroad for ever increasing periods of time; these are only some of the many factors that have now led many children of five to ten years old to learn to adapt themselves to frequent periods of having a parent away from home. This affects children under five as well, but parents tend to feel less restrained in their movements when the child starts full time school.

When a 5–10-year-old shows signs of distress (nightmares, tummy pains, crying episodes, or other complaints that lead him to cling anxiously to the mother) that appear to be related to his father's absence, it can be difficult to establish the precise dynamics of the child's feelings towards each of his parents. If we assume that it is father who travels abroad and mother who stays home (for the sake of brevity, I will use this configuration in the following discussion), some children feel angry at the father for abandoning them, others feel angry with the mother for having sent father away, others feel guilty that they may have done something that led father to depart, others feel scared that father will never come back, and still others become terrified lest the mother also leaves them. And, indeed, these are not mutually exclusive possibilities. But the average 5–10-year-old may find it very difficult to articulate the questions or comments that might enable the mother to know what feelings and ideas lie behind his distress.

When father has work commitments that demand his absence from home for hours or days, the child will obviously tend to rely more on his mother's ministrations. If mother is happy with her husband's absences, this situation will usually pose few or no problems. If, however, she resents his being away for prolonged intervals, this may influence the way in which she deals with the child's reactions to the situation. When this happens, it makes a difference whether mother and child have other members of the wider family to whom to turn for support or whether they are left to count only on each other.

I have never truly worked out what leads one parent to seek professional help, while another one who seems to be in precisely the same situation will be unable to look for this source of help. I definitely do not mean that only a professional can help a distressed parent, but there are moments when the relative, colleague, or friend who has been helpful in the past turns out not to be available or, for some reason, is not able or willing to help. If this is a mother who feels let down by a husband or partner and now finds her child too demanding, it can be very disheartening when she does not succeed in mobilizing a usually reliable source of support. The child will almost certainly sense the mother's resulting sense of isolation and helplessness, and this adds a further complex set of feelings to those already experienced by the child.

It is very intriguing to discover that many 5–10-year-olds will not ask questions about the absent father. This does not mean that they have forgotten him, and quite often the lack of questions may follow the child's impression that such questions give rise to strong feelings of distress in the mother. Observing the daily home life of a family in these circumstances is a totally different experience from meeting them in a consulting room, where, by definition, we are dealing with a child who has shown feelings or behaviour that the parent(s) cannot help or cope with.

It is to be hoped that the child in the consulting room may give clues to the conscious and unconscious anxieties he is struggling with, and this is bound to be helpful to both the child and the parents. The child may, for example, express fears that the absent parent may not simply be fulfilling some work commitment, but in fact exploring the possibility of a final, definite departure. This should help the parents to realize how the child is interpreting the father's absences as clues to understanding the solidity or otherwise of the parents' relationship with each other, and this can give them a pointer as to how to discuss further absences with the child.

While the under-five or the pre-adolescent will often come out into the open with their thoughts about father's absences, sometimes voicing their relief or their sense of betrayal and abandonment, the 5–10-year-old tends to be far more reserved regarding his feelings about the father's absence. Good sense would dictate that, even without emotional crises, it can only be useful that the mother should bring up the subject of the father's absence and not only explore the child's feelings, but also convey the message that he will come back. This is not difficult when the mother feels happy with the father's behaviour. When, however, phone calls, letters or e-mail messages suddenly cease for any significant length of time, it is quite possible that the mother resents that silence or harbours more serious concerns and this will, obviously, influence the way in which the child will be addressed.

On a more practical level, assuming we have a father who goes abroad for a rather lengthy period and the mother is left to look after their child(ren), it is virtually certain that sooner or later one of the children will come to the mother's bed and ask for permission to sleep there. This is a simple issue when the mother feels confident and in control of domestic life, but when she is depressed or feeling lonely, it can be tempting to have the warm reassurance of a loving child lying next to her. Following recommendations made earlier (see "sleeping problems", p. 67), it is important not to risk turning this request into a nightly ritual.

Before finishing this chapter, perhaps I should make explicit an assumption that underlies much of what was written above. We now live in an age where marriage is no longer the rule to rubber-stamp the legitimacy of a relationship. Whatever the people involved may argue, an informal relationship of any kind is bound to be taken as a kind of open door for the partners to act on any change of the feelings that originally brought them together. It cannot be only a coincidence that the number of divorces and separations has increased over the past decades, at the same time as the number of formal marriages has also decreased. Our present day 5–10-year-olds live in a world where there are too many children being brought up by a single parent and it is, therefore, not surprising that any clash between the parents should be taken by the child as a sign of possibly serious trouble. When it then happens that father has to leave home to travel abroad, the anxiety level of the child is bound to rise.

When our 5–10-year-old goes to his new school, he will soon make contact with one or more children who describe living with one parent during the week and then spending the weekend with the other parent. It is important to bear this in mind if, in the course of some innocent argument with your spouse, your child suddenly puts a question to you using the word "divorce". By the age of five, every child will have learnt how his parents address each other— not just what words they use, but the tone of voice and so many elements of what we call "body language". Whatever the frequency of these arguments and whatever the intensity of the clash, if the child has come to find that sooner or later peace returns and his parents treat each other lovingly, or at least amicably, the level of his anxiety when the next "match" is started will probably be quite manageable. But meeting children from divorced parents will add the image of a potential different outcome to his parents' rows: not just a couple of unhappy, sulking, resentful, tense people, but people who can actually decide to move away from each other— permanently.

Periods of marital conflict present difficulties for both parents, and when this is happening they may find it almost impossible to bear in mind the needs of their children. It is not just a question of the children's ages, but the much more elusive importance of their personality. One child will cry, another one will go silent, a third one may go off to his room "to study", another will "take sides" and address the parent seen to be "the tormentor"—there are endless possibilities. In most such situations, the marital conflict takes on a different format and we suddenly have each parent reacting in opposite ways to the child's signs of distress. Understandable, no doubt, but still regrettable, since we then have a child who feels understood, loved, and protected by one parent and attacked by the other parent. The solution is easy: marital conflicts should be fought out, sorted out, in private, away from the children. Easy? Not really . . . It is precisely the impossibility of sparing the children from the pain of having divorced parents that leads to the repeated accusations that each parent raises against the other when the marital relationship appears unsustainable: "If this is how you see our relationship, why did you decide we should have children?" The wisdom of hindsight, sadly.

CHAPTER SIXTEEN

Illness and death

The subject of children with a permanent developmental handicap is discussed in another book in the present series (by Sheila and Martin Hollins). In the present chapter, the focus will be the ordinary illnesses that befall every 5–10-year-old and the problems related to the death of a close person.

In the course of my professional life, I have come to realize that each person has his own notion of what death means. It is not rare to find people who reach their adult life with no experience of losing a close person through death. Of course, they have a clear, definite, intellectual concept of death, but not having been through the direct impact of the loss of a dear one, they are spared the emotional turmoil and many of the anxieties that befall the person who had to cope with the experience of being alive while a dear person died.

Those brought up in a religious family will acquire very early the knowledge of death, in the context of heaven or hell taking over someone who lived on earth. But this is not quite the same as enjoying the company of a loved one and suddenly learning that he has fallen ill and may be harbouring a fatal condition or, worse still, finding that this person has died through an accident or an acute fatal illness. Our 5–10-year-old is particularly vulnerable to these traumatic experiences. Under-fives usually have a narrower concept of time, and the parallel notions of continuity and survival of the loved ones who are part of his world are simply taken for granted. By the age of five, the child has a much clearer notion of who belongs to his universe and has learnt about circumstances and time intervals that mark their appearance and departure. Learning that a loved one has died will always represent a traumatic experience for the child, but, putting his feelings under the microscope, we can find that the particular death is not usually seen as an isolated, self-contained loss, but as a warning that humans are fragile and other loved ones might also disappear. The child will also notice the pain he sees in parents and other members of the family, all combining to compose a picture of insecurity and unpredictability.

If the family have just been exposed to the death of a close member, it is important to be alert to any changes in the behaviour of the 5–10-year-old. When they ask explicit questions, it is not too difficult to find an answer, but it is important to restrict these answers to the specific content of the question. If, instead of clear questions, the child presents behaviour changes, it may be more difficult to enable the child to voice the reason for his anxiety. At such times, trying to comfort a 5–10-year-old who has woken up from a nightmare or who complains of being afraid of what might happen if he were to fall asleep, it is important to explore with him what thoughts and fears is he struggling with. Simple, universal, all-encompassing words of reassurance may not be sufficient to comfort and reassure the child.

Perhaps I should mention the awkward problem of how to deal with the child at the time of the burial. This may be one of those unavoidable occasions where the child's needs and wishes cannot be given priority. Some children, and, in fact, many adults, experience a powerful (conscious or unconscious) need to see the dead body of a loved one. Not seeing it, for whatever reason, leaves these people with a deep sense of doubt about whether that person has *really* died, and it is not rare to find them entertaining many fantasies to explain the reason why they can no longer meet the one who died; in other words, only seeing the actual dead body would allow them to accept that person's departure.

At the time of the funeral, all the adults are trying to cope with their pain and, rightly or wrongly, many of them cannot tolerate the presence of young children. Their reasons for this are not relevant, since what is involved is a highly charged situation that does not really allow for arguments or any attempts at persuading them to be reasonable. If parents and relatives feel comfortable about the child being present at the burial and other ceremonies, then this is appropriate, but only when the child involved is mature enough to cope with the experience. Taking a naïve five-year-old to a funeral ceremony in order to familiarize him with such occasions is not really justifiable. To describe the occasion as "an opportunity to say good-bye to grandpa" is, to my mind, not entirely fair to that naïve child's level of comprehension of life. But, if the whole family ethos involves children being present at funerals, this is quite a different proposition. The child's attendance is only one of many other examples of his progress within the ethical philosophy of the family into which he was born.

The ordinary life of non-religious families also contains various reminders of what death signifies for the survivors. Pictures of dead relatives are not rare, and occasionally candles will be lit on anniversaries. What can you say when your 5–10-year-old queries who or what is being remembered? It is not difficult to hear the answer in one's head, but it is not easy to decide what exactly to tell your child. "He has gone to heaven" is perhaps the most common answer, and it tends to satisfy most children. A more inquisitive 5–10-year-old may want to know more and, at this point, much depends on your personal feelings about that person and how you feel about losing him/her. I believe it is important that you respect your feelings. However mature and intelligent your 5–10-year-old, he will be very aware of your feelings and these are bound to be more important to him than the literal terms of your answer. The chances are that as long as you appear to be in control of your feelings, your 5–10-year-old will take the opportunity to ask you some of the questions he may have kept under cover, not certain that he could actually articulate them.

The past few generations have grown up knowing that many of the Holocaust survivors were unable and/or unwilling to tell their children of the experiences they had gone through. Many, not all, of the children involved eventually discovered what had happened to their elders and some of them have written of their feelings about this. These accounts show their attempts to understand the motives that led the parents to spare their offspring from the horrors of the war experiences, but there is also a tone of resentment, as if the parents had not trusted the children's capacity to share their pain. Of course, Holocaust survivors had an extraordinarily powerful tragedy to cope with and most of them struggled with their memories for the rest of their lives. To state the obvious, death is always traumatic, but the circumstances of the loss and the details involved in the process of dying can be even more painful than the actual, final *dénouement*. Being a part of these developments leaves the survivor with a multitude of terrible feelings that demand great courage to overcome. And each individual, whatever his age, has to find his own way of coping with the loss, and with the fact of remaining alive.

Moving to an entirely different field, we find families that lose a child during pregnancy, at birth, or early in life: how can they cope with this loss? Some couples choose to embark on a new pregnancy and this is sometimes referred to as having "a replacement child". I have actually met someone who told me that he had been given the same name as a sibling who had died a couple of years before his birth. Such findings have always made me wonder what leads parents to tell their children of these losses. Does this information help the child? What can the child make of this knowledge?

> A nine-year-old was brought to see me because of a protracted physical illness that the doctors had diagnosed as ME (myalgic encephalopathy). I was told that, in fact, his father had been given the same diagnosis for his physical complaints. In the course of the consultation, he was able to draw the members of his family and, when I queried a figure that had not been named by him or his parents up to that point, he told me that this was a child who had died in infancy. The parents were surprised that the boy should have remembered this, let alone mentioned it to me. I asked the boy "But what does this mean to you?" and, as he burst out crying, he said, "If he had lived, I would not have been born . . ."

> It happened that, in spite of the doctors' words of reassurance regarding the father's illness, the parents were concerned that this might, in fact, be a more serious condition and the family atmosphere contained the air of depression and hopelessness that had probably afflicted it

when their child had died. Certainly, at the consultation, both parents were surprised and immensely upset when their son revealed how intense were the feelings of living and dying that he was dealing with.

I would assume that these feelings were completely unconscious, since there was no suggestion that these thoughts existed in the boy's consciousness. But the sudden discovery of what his drawing meant seems to have helped the boy and the parents to face the possibility that the illnesses affecting father and son contained this unconscious dread of impending death.

I believe this discovery in our meeting helped the family to recognize, so to say, what belonged where. Two weeks later, I received a letter from the boy describing how much better he felt and that he had resumed his normal school life.

It does seem that many of the parents who lose a child tell their children (already born or those born subsequently) of the circumstances of the loss. I remember a friend telling me that, since her early childhood, she was familiar with a collection of photos that her mother kept on a shelf. She knew who the people were, but one of them depicted a child she could not identify. Incredible as it might seem, it was only after her mother died that she managed to ask her father about this picture and was then told that this was a child of theirs who had died a couple of years before my friend was born. Of course, it is possible that this person had, in fact, asked her mother about the picture and simply suppressed the memory of her mother's answer, but I find it equally possible that she sensed that this photo still represented a source of pain to the mother and refrained from upsetting her.

Children can only make sense of what they learn according to the level of comprehension they have reached at that time. Under-fives will repeat words they have heard about death, but I believe that they grasp no more than the fact that the parent(s) who told them of this had been through an experience of pain that was still affecting them. After five or six years of age, children are likely to know more about separation and absence and whether these lead to a reassuring return or to a permanent loss. Even so, it is totally unpredictable what the child will eventually elaborate from the information he is given and how these interpretations will affect him.

After all these comments about the child's reaction to information that he may not really understand, I should make it clear that, in my view, the most important element in these situations is the emotional experience of the parents. As already stated many times, I strongly believe that children can sense a parent's emotional state. But it is very rare for a 5–10-year-old to ask the parent for *the reason* for his anxiety. They may say, "Oh, Mummy . . . you are upset today!", but it is not common that they should ask, "Oh, Mummy, why are you upset?". The more common reaction is for the 5–10-year-old to come up with some piece of behaviour that is meant to divert the parent's attention from whatever might be making them anxious. In other words, the child finds it easier (and kinder!) to have an angry parent than a sad, anxious one.

What about the child suffering from an illness? Little ones struggle with whatever causes them pain and discomfort and are quite able to protest when the treatment involves injections or medication that has unpleasant tastes: they will cry, throw themselves around, have tantrums . . . the variations are endless. But the over-five (and younger, but more mature little ones) will be affected not only by the physical symptoms of the disease, but also by what their imagination builds over the symptoms and, more subtle, by what interpretation they place on the parents' reaction to their state. Unfortunately, what the doctor says is never enough to completely reassure a worried parent.

There was a time in the long-lost past that most families had a doctor who looked after all its members for many years. We now have to rely on busy GPs or specialists who tend to concentrate on the particular body part in which they specialize. Occasionally, a family is fortunate enough to discover a paediatrician who takes into account not only the child's body, but also his personality and, even more important, the parents' reaction to the child's illness. Let us consider a seven-year-old girl who cannot get rid of a cough that sometimes leads to the expectoration of some catarrh, but most of the time is just unpleasantly dry and unproductive. Antibiotics produce improvement, but soon enough the cough is back. Various cough medicines also produce some improvement, but no cure. Time and again the paediatrician tries to convince the parents that they should ignore the girl's cough, but it happens that the paternal grandfather died of lung cancer and a distant cousin of the mother was found to suffer from tuberculosis. How can these parents be completely reassured that their daughter has an unpleasant but not serious cough? If the paediatrician is prepared to ask the parents the relevant questions that might bring to the surface the true cause of their worries, he might be able to reassure them, but not many doctors are able or willing to do this.

We must recognize that it is difficult to be a parent, particularly when your child gets ill. When the illness is not serious and clears in a short period of time, life just goes on. The only danger that parents must bear in mind is that the child can pick up any anxiety that their illness arouses in the parents and this can lead to what (regrettably) many people describe as "attention-seeking behaviour" (see p. 96). But we are only human, and it is quite pointless to tell a parent that he need not worry about his child's illness.

Unfortunately, we have children who do develop serious and even fatal illnesses. The 5–10-year-old will soon realize when his illness is considered serious and requires special treatment, particularly if he has to be admitted to hospital. These will be difficult times for the whole family, and it is important, absolutely vital, that both parents should unite and help each other to cope with this dreaded scenario. The sick child will need help and any siblings will also require considerable help. And, equally important, the parents will also do well to find someone who may be prepared to hold their hands through the crisis.

When a family is struck by the tragedy of a seriously ill child, there is no shortage of people ready to give them advice. Parents will recognize that these people are well intentioned, but this is certainly not the kind of help they need. Parents are struggling with a loss of hope, and having people trying to convince them that they must not lose hope is not what will bring that hope back. I believe that the best help one can give to a parent in this position is to give them a chance to find the words to describe their despair. It does not really matter whether you give advice or make noises to indicate you are hearing them, the all-important challenge is to convey your sense of appreciating the helplessness and the horrendous pain the parents feel because of not being able to help their child.

What to tell the child who is struck by a serious or fatal illness? Much depends on the personality and intelligence of the child. The challenge is to fathom out what the child himself makes of his situation. To tell him what you, the parent, make of it is likely to be no more than a repeat of what doctors and nurses have been telling him, anyway. Some hospitals do count on psychologists or counsellors or specialized nurses who will try to help the child to voice his fears and, in such circumstances, it is best to have a meeting with these professionals, to make sure that you follow the same approach. If there is no such professional available, the best approach is to convey to the child that you want to hear his thoughts about his situation. Words of reassurance will be important, but the parent should be guided by the child's words. If the child voices words of hope and confidence, this should be confirmed and reinforced. If the child voices words of fear and dread, this should not be denied or corrected; if at all possible, it may be helpful to convey how his pain is shared by his loved ones, but then put into words shared past experiences that were enjoyed and remembered by them as symbols of their mutual love.

Sometimes the sick child may ask questions about the future, his own and that of the surviving ones. Parents will certainly find it difficult to contain their tears and discover words to put forward. If they can muster the self-control required, they may say that whatever their future life, that child will always be present and, who knows?, perhaps he will be watching them from somewhere and what a shame that those living may not be able to hear what he makes of their ventures, but they will certainly try to guess what his opinions are: after all, they know him well enough to raise such guesses! The message here is that "remembering him" are not just empty words, but a reference to how much they have absorbed and will remember of his way of thinking and being.

Some children will enjoy being reminded of occasions when their participation was particularly meaningful. Other children may come up with accounts that the parents find silly, irrelevant, or just irritating—this must be taken as an indication of how that child feels at that particular moment. Yes, such stories may be a denial of the underlying despair, but, if at all possible, the parents should allow the child to have his respite and, therefore, be careful not to correct him or try to change the flow of the conversation.